BLACK AND MINORITY ETHNIC HOUSING STRATEGIES: A GOOD PRACTICE GUIDE

BOB BLACKABY AND KUSMINDER CHAHAL

CHARTERED INSTITUTE OF HOUSING
FEDERATION OF BLACK HOUSING ORGANISATIONS
THE HOUSING CORPORATION

The Chartered Institute of Housing

The Chartered Institute of Housing is the professional organisation for all people who work in housing. Its purpose is to take a strategic and leading role in encouraging and promoting the provision of good quality affordable housing for all. CIH has 16,000 members working in local authorities, RSLs, the private sector and educational institutions.

Chartered Institute of Housing
Octavia House
Westwood Way
Coventry CV4 8JP
Tel: 024 7685 1700 Fax: 024 7669 5110
Website: www.cih.org

Federation of Black Housing Organisations

FBHO is a radical and practical organisation that works with members and key partners to promote, support and develop a vibrant and dynamic black and minority ethnic social housing sector by providing quality services based on campaigning, research and project development.

Federation of Black Housing Organisations
Basement Offices
137 Euston Road
London NW1 2AA
Tel: 020 7388 1560 Fax: 020 7383 0613
Website: www.fbho.co.uk

The Housing Corporation

The Housing Corporation is the government agency which registers, regulates and funds over 2,000 social landlords in England, which between them provide around one million homes for people in need. The Corporation has an important role as a promoter of good practice in the social housing sector.

The Housing Corporation
149 Tottenham Court Road
London W1P 0BN
Tel: 020 7393 2000 Fax: 020 7393 2111
Website: www.housingcorp.gov.uk

Black and Minority Ethnic Housing Strategies: A Good Practice Guide
Written by Bob Blackaby and Kusminder Chahal
Commissioning editor: Sarah Edwards
Editor: Jane Allanson

© Chartered Institute of Housing, Federation of Black Housing Organisations and The Housing Corporation, 2000
ISBN: 1 900396 64 5

Design by Jeremy Spencer
Cover illustration by Liz Pichon
Printed by: Hobbs the Printers, Totton

CONTENTS

FOREWORD

A message from the Minister of State for Housing and Planning

It is vitally important for local authorities and their partners to take full account of the needs and aspirations of black and minority ethnic communities in their area when drawing up their housing strategies.

Recognising diversity is the essential first step to developing a strategy. Successful and sustainable strategies will reflect the priorities of local people, so there is no standard approach. This Guide provides step-by-step advice on how authorities and their partners can develop the best strategy to meet local circumstances. Building on the experience of a wide range of organisations, there are examples throughout so that readers can see how suggestions have been put into practice.

Successful partnership is essential throughout every stage of developing and implementing a strategy - local authorities, consumers, BME community organisations, local RSLs, and the voluntary sector all have a role to play. Similarly, the BME housing strategy does not operate in a vacuum, but requires active links with related local strategies such as corporate efforts to tackle anti-poverty, crime and disorder.

I am delighted to have been asked to make a contribution. I welcome and fully endorse the joint working between the Federation of Black Housing Organisations, the Chartered Institute of Housing and the Housing Corporation to produce this Guide. I would also encourage all housing organisations to make full use of the Guide to ensure that they take into account the needs and requirements of BME communities.

Nick Raynsford

Nick Raynsford MP

About the Authors

Bob Blackaby
Bob is a freelance housing consultant. He has over 25 years experience in housing, much of it in local government. His specialisms include the assessment of housing requirements, policy development and race and equalities work. Bob has worked in mainstream housing management and has had university research and teaching experience. He is a fellow of the Chartered Institute of Housing.

Kusminder Chahal
Kusminder joined the Ethnicity and Health Unit at the University of Central Lancashire in 1998 after completing a national research project on the impact and consequences of racist harassment. He has worked as a social researcher since graduating from the University of Bristol (MSc, Race Relations) in 1991, and has undertaken a variety of research projects. Kusminder is currently involved in research looking at the effectiveness of community-based anti-racist harassment support projects.

ACKNOWLEDGEMENTS

The Chartered Institute of Housing and the Federation of Black Housing Organisations would like to thank the Housing Corporation for funding the research, writing and production of this Guide through its Innovation and Good Practice (IGP) Grant programme. Funding from the National Assembly for Wales for work on the surveys is also gratefully acknowledged.

Harris Beider of the FBHO and Kurshida Mirza and David Cheesman of the Housing Corporation provided helpful support, advice and guidance throughout the project.

The following people gave their time to read and comment on the text at various stages, and their feedback was invaluable:

Anne Marie Andreoli	Home Office
Pete Bailey	Rochdale MBC
Louise Barnden	Chartered Institute of Housing in Wales/ Riviera HA
Jan Bird	DETR
Sharon Carter	Frontline Housing Advice Ltd.
Jo Charlesworth	Commission for Racial Equality
Alan Ferguson	Chartered Institute of Housing in Scotland
David Fotheringham	Chartered Institute of Housing
Robert Fox	DETR
Abdul Jabbar	Rochdale MBC
Gary Messenger	DETR
Reena Mukherji	Presentation HA
Robina Qureshi	Positive Action in Housing
Melanie Rees	Chartered Institute of Housing
Marian Reid	Chartered Institute of Housing
Kulbir Shergil	Bristol City Council
Rhian Thomas	Chartered Institute of Housing in Wales
Richard Tomlins	De Montfort University
Marie Vernon	Chartered Institute of Housing
Purnima Wilkinson	Leicester City Council
Helen Williams	National Housing Federation
Jeanette York	Local Government Association
Patrick Yu	Northern Ireland Council for Ethnic Minorities

Thanks are also due to the local authorities which completed and returned the survey questionnaires, and to all the organisations which provided good practice examples and discussed their initiatives with the authors.

CHAPTER 1

INTRODUCTION

This chapter outlines:
- The background to, and contents of, this Guide
- The legal responsibilities of local authorities and other bodies regarding race equality
- The implications of the Lawrence Inquiry report
- The Commission for Racial Equality codes of practice
- Requirements for registered social landlords (RSLs)
- Best Value guidance and its implications for race equality
- The work of the Social Exclusion Unit on tackling the social exclusion faced by many black and minority ethnic communities

The report of the inquiry into the death of Stephen Lawrence has, once again, put the spotlight on 'race' in this country. The report's recommendations challenge those in positions of authority and influence to take decisive steps to tackle racism and discrimination. Work in the field of housing should be a vital component of this programme of action.

More recently, the National Strategy for Neighbourhood Renewal and the work of the Social Exclusion Unit (SEU) has highlighted the work required to tackle the disproportionate social exclusion experienced by some people from black and minority ethnic communities. The report *Minority Ethnic Issues in Social Exclusion and Neighbourhood Renewal* (SEU, 2000d) details the nature and effect of the exclusion of black and minority ethnic communities and recommends what must be done in a range of fields to further tackle race inequality.

This Guide aims to ensure that race equality is central to the way in which local authorities, registered social landlords and other organisations, develop and implement their local housing strategies. It sets out the importance of developing local black and minority ethnic housing strategies in partnership with the communities themselves and with a range of other organisations.

The Housing Corporation's *Black and Minority Ethnic Housing Policy* emphasises the importance of partnership working in delivering culturally competent services to black and minority ethnic communities. The policy encourages registered social landlords to work with local authorities to develop and implement black and minority ethnic strategies.

The National Assembly for Wales has commissioned research into the need for a black and minority ethnic housing strategy for Wales. The project report includes a recommendation that the National Assembly takes a strategic approach to identifying and meeting black and minority ethnic housing needs as part of its overall housing strategy for Wales (Nyoni, 2000).

Scottish Homes' race equality strategy was first launched in 1994. The strategy is under review, with a revised document to be published later in 2000.

This Guide aims to be of practical help to all of those who are responsible for developing strategies or providing services within local housing organisations. It builds on the general guidance given in the CIH/LGA Good Practice Guide on *Designing Local Housing Strategies* (Goss and Blackaby, 1998).

Readers of this Guide are encouraged to consider ways in which housing organisations can fulfil their responsibilities to ensure race equality in the policies they operate and provide services that are sensitive to the needs that exist within the diverse communities they serve. As such, the Guide aims to be of use to all housing organisations throughout the United Kingdom: local authorities, registered social landlords or other bodies, such as housing action trusts.

Chapter 2 is written from the perspective of local authorities and concerns the compilation of local and black and minority ethnic strategies. However, much of what is in the chapter should be useful to all of those who are seeking to devise a policy for race equality within their organisations. The chapter emphasises that local authorities should fully involve partner organisations in the development of local strategies. Chapter 6 returns to the theme of partnership working, including partnerships between local authorities and RSLs.

Chapters 3, 4, 5 and 7 are aimed at all housing organisations. Parts of chapter 4 concern local authorities' strategic role but will also be of interest to strategic partners, particularly RSLs.

A summary of the contents of each chapter is set out below:

- Chapter 2 contains guidance about the process of compiling a black and minority ethnic housing strategy
- Chapter 3 sets out how housing organisations should provide a framework for race equality in services and employment
- Chapter 4 examines race equality issues in relation to the strategic role of local authorities. It also discusses ways in which housing organisations can incorporate race equality principles in the services they provide to the wider community
- Chapter 5 discusses how organisations managing housing should aim for race equality in the services they provide to tenants and potential tenants
- Chapter 6 examines good practice in relation to joint work between local authorities, RSLs, voluntary organisations and contractors
- Chapter 7 discusses monitoring and evaluation

Examples of current good practice and the results from a postal survey of local authorities are included at various points throughout the Guide. The survey shows that, although many authorities are taking steps to promote race equality in the services they provide, there are others that need to make considerable progress. It is hoped that this Guide will stimulate the organisations that have already made a start to refine their approaches to meeting the diverse needs of their communities, as well as to act as a spur to those that are still some way behind.

❏ Requirements and expectations for housing organisations

Housing organisations, as well as responding to the requirements of the local communities they serve, have to ensure they are meeting their legal obligations, their regulators' expectations and the expectations arising from specific national agendas for change as set out below.

■ Legal requirements

Race Relations Act 1976

The Race Relations Act 1976 places various duties on housing providers to eliminate racial discrimination and promote equality of opportunity. The Act introduces the key concepts of direct and indirect discrimination and sets out when it is lawful for positive action to be taken to provide services specifically for particular ethnic groups.

- **Accommodation and services**
  - Section 20 states that 'it is unlawful for any persons concerned with the provision (for payment or not) of goods, facilities and services to the public or a section of the public to discriminate against a person who seeks to obtain or use those goods, facilities or services.'
  - Section 21 outlaws discrimination in the disposal and management of premises and applies to all non-resident landlords.
- **Duty to promote equality of opportunity**
  - Under section 71 of the Race Relations Act, local authorities and certain other public sector bodies are required 'to make appropriate arrangements with a view to securing that their various functions are carried out with due regard to the need to eliminate unlawful discrimination and to promote equality of opportunity and good relations between persons of different racial groups.'
- **Positive action**
  - Section 35 of the Race Relations Act allows for positive action to be taken to provide services for particular racial groups. This takes the form of a general exemption from the provisions of the Act for 'any act done in affording persons of a particular racial group access to facilities or services to meet the special needs of persons of that group in regard to their education, training or welfare, or any ancillary benefits.'

Northern Ireland Act 1998
Section 75 of the Northern Ireland Act 1998 requires public authorities carrying out their functions relating to Northern Ireland to have regard to the need to promote equality of opportunity between people of different religious belief, political opinion, racial group, age, marital status or sexual orientation. The Act requires public bodies to prepare Equality Schemes stating how they propose to fulfil the new duties. These schemes must be submitted for approval to the new Equality Commission for Northern Ireland.

The Commission has issued guidelines on Public Authority Equality Schemes to help organisations to comply with the new legislative requirements.

Amendments to the Race Relations Act
The government is proposing to introduce important changes to the law through its Race Relations (Amendment) Bill. The new legislation will extend the provisions on direct and indirect discrimination and victimisation to all functions of specified public authorities, including central and local

government and the police. The law will also be amended to place a duty to promote race equality on a wider range of public authorities.

■ Implications of the inquiry following the death of Stephen Lawrence

The Lawrence Inquiry report was published on 24 February 1999 (Macpherson, 1999). The report stressed the part played by institutional racism in the investigation by the Metropolitan Police Service of Stephen Lawrence's murder. The Inquiry defined institutional racism as:

> *'The collective failure of an organisation to provide an appropriate and professional service to people because of their colour, culture or ethnic origin. It can be seen or detected in processes, attitudes and behaviour which amount to discrimination through unwitting prejudice, ignorance, thoughtless and racist stereotyping which disadvantage minority ethnic people'* (paragraph 6.34)

Institutional racism is a problem for the whole of any organisation. To begin to tackle the problem, everyone in all organisations needs to ask some fundamental questions, for example:

- Do we understand the diverse needs of black and minority ethnic communities?
- Do our services meet the diverse needs and aspirations of black and minority ethnic communities?
- Do we provide an 'appropriate and professional service' to black and minority ethnic communities?
- Do we achieve equally high outcomes for all ethnic groups in all our activities?

For housing providers, the report is a clear reminder that having a strategic response is important in translating policies into practice. This can only be achieved through clear lines of management and responsibility, training for employees, monitoring and evaluation of the effectiveness of policies, community consultation and effective disciplinary procedures.

■ Commission for Racial Equality codes of practice

The Commission for Racial Equality (CRE) has issued codes of practice for the promotion of race equality and prevention of discrimination in the areas of employment, rented housing and non-rented (owner-occupied) housing. Although these codes do not have statutory force, they can be used as evidence in court proceedings.

With regard to service delivery, the CRE code of practice in rented housing recommends:

- Implementation of an equal opportunities policy, giving particular attention to training staff and ensuring that the services provided are understood by clients
- Keeping ethnic records and monitoring systems, including information on the nature of the enquiry or problem, and its outcome. This data should serve as a source of information on the needs of the various communities, and should be analysed to ensure that services are being provided in an equitable way.

Within the Audit Commission's performance indicators framework, local authorities in England and Wales are required to say whether they follow the code of practice in rented housing.

■ Expectations for RSLs

The Housing Corporation's Performance Standards for RSLs set out its expectations of RSLs in England. The Corporation launched its black and minority ethnic housing strategy in May 1998. The objective of the policy is to develop in RSLs a culture which empowers black and minority ethnic communities and which integrates their needs and aspirations into RSLs' everyday business. To demonstrate compliance with the regulatory regime, RSLs' governing bodies must confirm that:

- They have and operate effective equal opportunities policies and procedures and review them regularly
- They review their performance against the CRE codes of practice for employment and rented housing
- They have a strategy to ensure that their policies, procedures and practices support the recruitment and retention of people from black and minority ethnic communities to committees and the workforce, and facilitate their progress to key decision-making positions
- They have a strategy to ensure that their management and development services respond to black and minority ethnic housing needs in the local authority areas in which they operate

Standards for RSLs in Scotland published by Scottish Homes and the Scottish Federation of Housing Associations (1999) state that landlords must have and operate policies and procedures which promote equal opportunities and which seek to eliminate unfair discrimination. Scottish Homes' revised race equality strategy, to be launched later in 2000, aims to include more robust systems for monitoring RSLs' performance in this area.

Regulations issued for RSLs in Wales by the former Tai Cymru (1997) state that RSLs should make sure there is no unfair discrimination on the basis of race, sex or disability in the provision of housing, services or employment. The regulations say that RSLs should take steps to identify unfair discrimination, take action to improve performance and ensure that their tenants are aware of their rights under equal opportunities legislation.

■ Housing Investment Programme Guidance for Local Authorities

The Housing Investment Programme (HIP) Guidance for English local authorities issued in 2000 addresses 'race' issues in Appendix A. In particular, it stresses:

- All local housing authorities should ensure that the needs and aspirations of black and minority ethnic people and communities form an integral part of the local housing strategy

- The importance of measuring housing need by ethnic breakdown in all housing needs assessments, with additional separate surveys of black and minority ethnic communities as required

- The importance of working with partners and stakeholders to meet black and minority ethnic housing needs, especially local communities and black-led RSLs

- The need for local housing authorities to demonstrate evidence of strategies to tackle discrimination and harassment

- That local authorities should adopt the Home Office *Code of Practice on the Reporting and Recording of Racist Incidents*

■ Best Value

Best Value seeks to modernise local government, raise standards and encourage competition and innovation. All local authorities have a duty to introduce Best Value arrangements and they are also to be applied to RSLs.

Under Best Value arrangements, organisations should conduct reviews of their services. The reviews should:

- **Challenge** why and how a service is provided

- **Compare** performance of others across a range of indicators

- **Consult** tax payers, service users, partners and the wider business community in the setting of targets

- Consider fair **competition** as a means of securing efficient and effective services

Government guidance to local authorities in England was issued in Circular 10/99 by the Department of the Environment, Transport and Regions (DETR) in December 1999. The guidance states that local authorities should engage with users and potential users on Best Value and efforts should be made to reach people who, traditionally, have been under-represented. The guidance goes on to say that equity considerations should be borne in mind, including the setting of targets to redress disparities in the provision of services to people who are socially, economically or geographically disadvantaged (DETR, 1999a). This message is endorsed in specific guidance on housing contained within the *Best Value in Housing Framework* (DETR, 2000a).

Best Value provides a good opportunity for local authorities and RSLs to review the appropriateness and quality of services to black and minority ethnic people and to make changes to their services where these are needed.

Under Best Value performance indicators, local authorities are now required to report on whether they have adopted the CRE's standard for local government and, if so, which level they have reached. There are five levels in all (DETR, 1999b; CRE, 1996).

■ The National Strategy for Neighbourhood Renewal

The Social Exclusion Unit, set up by the Prime Minister in 1997 to improve the co-ordination of government action to tackle social exclusion, identified the need for a national strategy to revitalise deprived neighbourhoods. The findings and recommendations of 18 Policy Action Teams are feeding in to the overall National Strategy for Neighbourhood Renewal. Some recommendations are already being taken forward while others are still under consideration. Many will provide an important framework for future work by housing organisations and their partners.

In relation to housing and race inequality, the National Strategy Framework and the Policy Action Teams recommend that:

- Every social landlord should adopt a written policy on race equality that reflects the CRE's Code of Practice and the National Housing Federation's Equality Code
- Local authorities, in focusing on creating and sustaining more mixed neighbourhoods, should ensure ethnic minorities have a choice in housing to avoid them becoming concentrated in the worst housing
- Local authorities should involve minority ethnic communities across all tenures in drawing up strategies for tackling areas of unpopular housing
- Regeneration models involving minority ethnic groups and faith groups should be piloted in some unpopular areas

(source: Social Exclusion Unit 2000d)

❏ Ethnic diversity

There is great diversity amongst the black and minority ethnic communities that live in the United Kingdom. This diversity stems from differences in demographic factors, such as age and household type, economic position, culture and expectations, experience, including the length of time in which communities have lived here, and current housing situation. The challenge for black and minority ethnic housing strategies is to recognise the diversity of needs and expectations, and the starting point must be the development of approaches to consultation that recognise this diversity.

The extent of diversity is likely to vary between areas and it is not always possible to apply the findings from consultation or research in one area to another area. Nevertheless, an examination of the existing body of research can be a useful springboard for more detailed work locally. The list of references at the end of this Guide contains a number of useful sources, including recent reports published by the Policy Studies Institute (Modood et al, 1997; Beishon, Modood and Virdee, 1998) and a number of studies about the needs of particular communites.

■ Disadvantage

While the experiences of different black and minority ethnic communities vary widely, the Social Exclusion Unit's work has drawn attention to the double disadvantage encountered by many people from these communities. This is explained as:

- Black and minority ethnic communities are disproportionately concentrated in deprived areas and suffer all the problems (eg relating to health, housing, education, access to training and employment) that affect other people in these areas

- In addition, people from black and minority ethnic communities also suffer the consequences of:
  - Overt and inadvertant racial discrimination – individual and institutional
  - An inadequate recognition and understanding of the complexities of minority ethnic groups, and hence services that fail to reach them or meet their needs
  - Additional barriers like language, cultural and religious differences

(source: Social Exclusion Unit 2000d)

❑ The Guide

■ Compiling the Guide

The compilation of this Guide has involved several stages of research:

- A postal questionnaire survey of all local authorities in England, Scotland and Wales. A total of 158 questionnaires were returned, which represents a response rate of 40%. The completed questionnaires represented a reasonable cross section of authorities in England, Scotland and Wales and of larger and smaller authorities, as well as authorities with larger and smaller concentrations of black and minority ethnic communities. The Welsh part of the survey was carried out in conjunction with the National Assembly for Wales and has been used to help the Assembly develop its approach to race equality.

- Compilation of good practice material. This involved considering reports and other documents submitted by local authorities and other organisations and follow-up telephone calls to obtain further information and to clarify the approach taken.

- A literature review. This provided an overall context to the research process and enabled the authors to bring a diverse range of materials together in the Guide.

■ Terminology used in the Guide

In this Guide, the term **black and minority ethnic** is used. The phrase 'black and minority ethnic people' includes Irish people in Britain and the traveller community.

The term **registered social landlord (RSL)** is used to mean housing associations, housing co-operatives and local housing companies.

Although some of this guide is addressed specifically to local authorities, much of the material will be relevant to a wider range of organisations, especially RSLs. Where this applies, the term **housing organisation** is used. The term is intended to cover local authorities, other statutory housing bodies (such as housing action trusts and the Northern Ireland Housing Executive), RSLs and voluntary organisations providing housing services.

This Guide uses the term **racist harassment** rather than 'racial harassment'. However, in some of the examples of good practice, some documents cited use the term 'racial harassment'. These references have been reproduced without amendment.

CHAPTER 2

DESIGNING A BLACK AND MINORITY ETHNIC HOUSING STRATEGY

This chapter discusses:

- Why local authorities should prepare black and minority ethnic housing strategies
- The process for compiling the strategy
- The contents of the strategy

❑ Why a black and minority ethnic housing strategy?

Local authorities have a legal obligation to carry out their functions in a way that eliminates unlawful discrimination and which promotes equality of opportunity and good race relations. In developing practical strategies to meet this and to ensure best practice and good customer care, local authorities need to tailor their services to be sensitive to differences in the needs and preferences of the various communities in the area. The development and implementation of a black and minority ethnic housing strategy is an invaluable tool in ensuring local authorities fulfil these requirements.

The basic principle underlying this Guide is that all local housing authorities should produce a clear written black and minority ethnic housing strategy. This document should explain and set out what the authority and its partners are seeking to achieve in terms of race equality in housing. The black and minority ethnic strategy should form an integral part of the local housing strategy.

More specifically, local authorities should implement and promote a black and minority ethnic housing strategy because:

- It will provide a framework for tackling racial discrimination and disadvantage
- It provides clarity to the authority, its partners and service users on what they are seeking to achieve in the field of race equality
- It demonstrates to black and minority ethnic communities the authority's commitment to race equality by setting out measurable objectives and performance targets that can be monitored in order to determine how far progress has been made
- The process of compiling the strategy can be a capacity-building one for staff within the authority and partner organisations, as well as for the communities themselves
- Focusing attention on methods of consultation, research and service provision for black and minority ethnic communities may trigger off improvements for other groups of service users, such as women or people with disabilities, or may serve to reinforce the importance of tackling social exclusion more generally

There are no hard and fast rules about the size and complexity of the strategy document. Some local authorities might choose to produce one overall housing strategy/housing plan/housing strategy and operational plan and then develop further documents which focus on specific issues. The key point is that each authority's black and minority ethnic housing strategy will be different because it will reflect the local situations prevailing in their area and the priorities of the communities they serve.

However, an action plan alongside the strategy is crucial. By breaking down large and long-term goals into achievable chunks the action plan should set out the targets against performance for the local authority and for all the partners involved, and should be regularly reviewed. Further, the strategy and action plan must clearly identify who has responsibility for developing, implementing and reviewing the strategy, with commitments secured both internally and externally. The most effective approach is for one named officer to have overall responsibility for co-ordinating and monitoring the action plan.

Further, the strategy should make clear that this is not a one-off task. The process of developing, promoting and implementing the strategy needs to be flexible and adaptable in response to the changing needs of black and minority ethnic communities.

> ## Survey results
>
> ### Black and minority ethnic housing strategies
>
> ✏ Across England, Scotland and Wales, only 18% of authorities have a written black and minority ethnic housing strategy. However, in districts where the black and minority ethnic population is 10% or more of the total, 43% of authorities have a written strategy.
>
> ✏ 43% of authorities with written black and minority ethnic housing strategies have presented them in 'stand alone' documents. In the remaining 57% of authorities, it is part of another document: in most cases, part of the housing strategy statement/housing plan/housing strategy and operational plan.
>
> ✏ The topics most frequently covered in black and minority ethnic housing strategies are: racist harassment, the investment programme of the authority and RSLs, access to housing, services to tenants/potential tenants and consultation and participation policies.
>
> ✏ Three quarters of black and minority ethnic strategies have links with wider social policies and programmes – the most frequently mentioned links were with anti-crime and community safety, regeneration and anti-poverty policies.
>
> ✏ Only a fifth of authorities set targets for the achievement of specified outcomes and outputs in relation to their black and minority ethnic strategy. Targets most frequently relate to tackling racist harassment, the provision of additional housing, consultation and participation and the letting of dwellings.

❏ Designing a black and minority ethnic housing strategy

The CIH/LGA Good Practice Guide *Designing Local Housing Strategies* sets out the main elements of an effective process for compiling a housing strategy. This is reproduced, with modifications, below.

> ### Main elements in designing an effective strategic process
>
> | | |
> |---|---|
> | Stage 1: | Designing the strategic process |
> | Stage 2: | Setting the strategic framework |
> | Stage 3: | Gathering information |
> | Stage 4: | Identifying the problems and determining intervention strategies |
> | Stage 5: | Option appraisal |
> | Stage 6: | Implementation |
> | Stage 7: | Monitoring and evaluation |

(Adapted from Goss and Blackaby, 1998, p.40)

■ Designing the strategic process

Getting the process right

Careful thought should be given to designing an effective process for drawing up a black and minority ethnic housing strategy. Inadequate data on the needs of black and minority ethnic communities may well result in a strategy which does not address key issues of inequality. A failure to consult properly may result in a document that does not reflect the communities' legitimate concerns, and the strategy may not be 'owned' by the key players. Neglecting to think about communication, implementation or monitoring may mean that, after it has been written, the strategy just stays on the shelf gathering dust.

Strategies must seek to achieve change:

> *'A good strategy should guide managerial action, focus energy, attention and resources, and help all staff and partners to understand what is intended to happen, and why'* (Goss and Blackaby, 1998, p. 42).

The following are essential conditions to a process that leads to change:

- A commitment to the strategy from the 'top' – from councillors, chief officers and senior managers

- An inclusive process – consultation with the communities themselves, with relevant people and organisations outside the authority, and with appropriate people from within, including front line staff, black and minority ethnic employees and staff from a range of disciplines and departments

- A clear analysis of the problems and options for solving them

- Full recognition of the diversity of the communities the organisation is seeking to serve and of the importance of tailoring services to meet the specific requirements of these communities

- A well written strategy document which clearly spells out what action is to be taken, by whom and when

- Good communication of the completed strategy, both within the authority and outside. All those charged with taking action need to know what is expected of them.

Involving stakeholders and black and minority ethnic communities

Full involvement of all the appropriate stakeholders and of local black and minority ethnic communities should ensure that the strategy reflects the key issues that are of concern to local people and that it is 'owned' by all the appropriate agencies responsible for its implementation.

There are three stages in strategy formulation where involvement is particularly important:

- In identifying the issues that need to be addressed
- In identifying solutions by setting objectives and appraising options
- Input into the draft strategy before it is finalised

There should also be opportunities later on, for example in helping to evaluate the success of the strategy.

Key people and organisations that need to be involved in developing the strategy include:

- **Community:**
  - People from the various black and minority ethnic communities, taking care to include people of different ages (especially younger people who may not otherwise get involved), women as well as men and people in all housing tenures and from the different areas within the district
  - Black and minority ethnic community representatives

- **Within the authority:**
  - Councillors
  - Staff involved in strategy, commissioning and service-providing roles in housing, social services/social work, planning, education, environmental services and economic development/regeneration departments
  - Personnel staff, who will be crucial in implementing the part of the strategy which is about employment and training
  - Black and minority ethnic employees

- **Partners and other organisations:**
  - Race Equality Council (REC) or equivalent
  - Anti-racist harassment projects and forums
  - Voluntary and community organisations which involve black and minority ethnic people
  - Black and minority ethnic service user groups, taking care to include young people and women
  - Where appropriate, county council staff with responsibilities for social services and education

- White-led and black and minority ethnic RSLs
- The Housing Corporation/Scottish Homes/National Assembly for Wales/Northern Ireland Housing Executive
- Housing advice centres
- The police
- Health authority/boards and trusts; primary health groups
- Local regeneration agencies
- Neighbouring local authorities, where there are likely to be cross-border issues
- Private landlords
- Estate agents
- Citizens' Advice Bureaux

RSLs are crucial partners, both as agencies that have a perspective on the needs and issues that should be addressed, and as organisations that will be involved in implementing the strategy. Many RSLs work across several local authority districts and will, therefore, need to contribute to more than one local black and minority ethnic housing strategy.

The role of the private rented sector as a strategic partner is sometimes overlooked. Private landlords and estate agents have an important role in ensuring black and minority ethnic communities have equal choice and access to housing.

The effective engagement of communities takes time, and efforts must be made to build up trust. This will be harder to achieve where expectations have been raised in the past but where no action has been taken. It is also likely to be difficult in areas of social tension, where some groups may be seen as having received more resources than other groups. These types of issues can be overcome with an open agenda, which aims to learn from past mistakes.

Overall, local authorities should not be afraid to learn from outside agencies and partners or to seek their advice. Further, it is important that authorities are honest with all partners and stakeholders about what can be achieved in the short term, and make it clear that some goals are long term but that the action plan shows how these will be achieved.

The diversity of cultures, and needs that exist within the communities, mean that a variety of approaches to involvement should be adopted. More detailed guidance on involving black and minority ethnic communities can be found in chapter 3.

Bristol City Council has produced a major race equality strategy for the period 2000 to 2004. It was drawn up in consultation with a range of organisations and people, including representatives from the Race Forum, which comprises people from black and minority ethnic communities within the city, black and minority ethnic RSLs, the Racial Equality Council and the Support Against Racist Incidents organisation.

The strategy document is arranged under six headings:
- Somewhere to live
- Achieving social inclusion
- Providing a safe environment
- Increasing economic wealth
- Working in partnership
- Working towards being a model employer

Each section includes a discussion of needs and current and future activities. A key part of the document is a series of targets. Some relate to performance, such as 'maintaining the figure of 30% take-up by black and minority ethnic households within group repair schemes'; 'where it has been agreed in cases of racist harassment, install an emergency alarm within five working days' and 'run a minimum of four anti-racism training courses a year'.

Other targets relate to service development. These include:
- Extend ethnic monitoring to include the quality of offers of accommodation and nominations to RSLs
- Provide a programme of training for area housing committees and tenants' groups on increasing black and minority ethnic tenant participation, race equality and tackling racial harassment
- Develop a positive action employee development scheme

An accompanying leaflet gives a brief guide to the strategy and is available in 10 other languages.

Progress in implementing the strategy will be monitored and reviewed by the Bristol Race and Housing Forum, which comprises representatives from the City Council, the Racial Equality Council, the Race Forum and the Bristol Housing Partnership.

Survey results

Formulating the black and minority ethnic housing strategy

- A third of authorities have specific mechanisms to consult with black and minority ethnic people when formulating their housing strategy or designing services or evaluating policies

- Consultative forums, ad hoc meetings and surveys were the most commonly used methods of consultation

- 55% of authorities have, in the last three years, made some assessment of the housing requirements of black and minority ethnic communities

- The most frequently used methods of assessment were: analysis of the waiting list and other records, analysis of Census data, interviews with representatives of black and minority ethnic organisations and surveys of black and minority ethnic households

- 30% of authorities have done some work to assess the needs of particular black and minority ethnic communities

---

Improving skills and understanding

Goss and Blackaby (1998) outline a number practical ways in which people can improve their 'strategic capacity' – the skills and understanding they need to help them prepare, implement and evaluate an effective local housing strategy. Methods include inter-departmental projects, joint conferences and forums and inter-agency training.

The process of involving stakeholders and the local community can itself be a capacity building experience. But before embarking on consultation excercises, those who are unfamiliar with the policy context or concepts such as 'direct' and 'indirect discrimination' or 'positive action' will need to address these issues.

Deciding how the strategy is to be communicated

The approach to communications needs to be broader than simple questions of the format of the finished document and whether it should be translated into other languages. The authority needs to decide:

- Who should be told about the intention to prepare the strategy

- Who needs to receive reports on progress throughout the process

- How the strategy itself is to be published, launched and disseminated

---

■ Setting the strategic framework

Boundaries

Geographical boundaries may need some thought. Generally, black and minority ethnic strategies cover the whole of a local authority district but their contents may need to reflect the fact that administrative and housing market boundaries often do not coincide. For example, there may be a great deal of movement of black and minority ethnic households between poor quality private housing in one district and that in another. Data collection exercises carried out to underpin the strategy will need to take account of this.

Scope

Strategies need to take account of the issues and problems that face local people and should therefore reflect the outcome of consultation exercises. Authorities should seek to cover the full range of black and minority ethnic communities that live in their districts. This is not to say that the needs of all of the communities have to be addressed in the same strategy document. In some authorities it may be appropriate to publish separate strategies for the various communities.

Linkages between housing and other corporate issues are of increasing importance. Local authorities are expected to take holistic approaches to problems and to develop housing strategies that have links with such issues as community regeneration and community care.

Some of the important linkages between black and minority ethnic strategies and corporate strategies are set out in the box on page 20.

Timescale

Decisions about the timescale of a black and minority ethnic strategy are a local matter. The strategy needs to allow enough time for things to change 'on the ground', but they should not become so out of date that they lose credibility. Three years is about the right length of time before a major review of the strategy is likely to be needed. Within the strategy, it is important to distinguish between long and short term goals. Regular progress reviews every two-three months will identify ahead of the annual review whether mechanisms or goals need to be changed.

Setting high level aims

High level aims should seek to encapsulate the authority's vision for race equality in housing. The aims need to be consistent with, and influenced by,

Examples of links between the black and minority ethnic housing strategy and other strategies

Strategy	Examples of links to black and minority ethnic housing strategy
Community regeneration	Decisions about where regeneration is to take place – do regeneration areas reflect areas where the most excluded black and minority ethnic communities live? Methods for consulting black and minority ethnic communities in regeneration areas. Support for black and minority ethnic businesses and community organisations
Community safety	Tackling racist harassment; crime reduction and making areas safer
Community care	Need for appropriate, culturally sensitive services to be provided by mainstream organisations. Need for targeted services for particular black and minority ethnic communities
Anti poverty	Benefit take-up campaigns targeted at particular minority communities; employment initiatives eg PATH
Older people	Culturally sensitive provision for older people from black and minority ethnic communities
Young people	Outreach work with black and minority ethnic youngsters on housing estates. Culturally sensitive services for young black and minority ethnic homeless people

the housing strategy and, where it exists, the authority's corporate race, or equal opportunities, strategy.

Aims of a black and minority ethnic housing strategy

- To eliminate unlawful racial discrimination
- To promote equal opportunities for all ethnic groups
- To deliver a high standard of service to people from black and minority ethnic communities within a framework of empowerment and Best Value
- To provide services that are sensitive to differences in needs, language and culture
- To recognise the diversity of local communities and to foster good relations between the communities
- To take positive action to address existing disadvantage and encourage a more inclusive society

---

■ Gathering Information

Building up a picture of the circumstances and views of black and minority ethnic people is a vital component of a black and minority ethnic housing strategy. As a starting point the local authority should plan an information gathering exercise to establish what are the priority local issues, and what mechanisms will be needed to ensure the community is part of the decision-making process in developing and implementing the strategy. Because of the diversity of needs and views within the black and minority ethnic communities, a number of different methods may be needed in order to ensure that data on the variety of circumstances and views are captured, and honest and open dialogues with the communities are established.

Assessing the needs of black and minority ethnic communities does not necessarily involve new pieces of research. Ethnic origin categories can be added to routine monitoring exercises in order to yield information about, for example, service take-up levels or service user satisfaction. General housing need surveys or tenant satisfaction surveys should also include ethnic origin questions so that data on needs and preferences of the various communities can be analysed.

Information on the following topics will be needed:

- Details of the current and projected future population and households, including breakdowns in terms of ethnicity, gender, age, household type and income

- The current housing circumstances of the black and minority ethnic communities, including tenure, type and size of dwelling, area, condition of dwelling, housing costs
- Housing needs and preferences of the various communities
- Levels of take-up by the various communities of current services
- Opinions about current services
- Social care, health, employment and education needs which housing providers need to take into account
- Racist harassment

Identifying black and minority ethnic needs

The London Borough of Croydon has worked in partnership with **Croydon People's Housing Association**, **Croydon Aashyana** project and **Cara Housing Association** to identify black and minority ethnic housing needs:

- **Croydon People's Housing Association**, a black and minority ethnic RSL, carried out a survey of black and minority ethnic housing needs in 1996/97. This was part funded by the council and the findings were discussed across various council departments. The results provided the centrepiece for a community based conference on Housing Plus initiatives in 1998 – again supported by the council and the Housing Corporation's Innovation and Good Practice Grant. The research has been written up as *Our Voices: A Community Consultation Report* (Croydon People's Housing Association, 1999).

- **Croydon Aashyana** project, which provides local housing mainly for elderly Asian women, completed a survey of Asian housing and related needs in the borough in 1997. It was funded jointly by the council, the Housing Corporation and Aashyana's parent housing association, Croydon Churches Housing Association. The council was involved in implementing some of the recommendations of this survey. One recommendation related to the requirement for an Asian Resource Centre.

- The council commissioned **Cara Housing Association**, an Irish RSL, to research Irish housing needs in Croydon in 1998. The project involved in-depth interviews with individuals and bringing together a number of focus groups. The report was launched in March 1999, raising the profile of the Irish community, and a number of recommendations are being implemented.

A number of initiatives have resulted from these projects, including the establishment of an organisation to develop the Asian Resource Centre. Other initiatives include council funding of a community development worker for Croydon People's Housing Association, a request from the council to all voluntary organisations to include Irish people within their ethnic monitoring of service delivery and an extensive 'diversity' training programme for council staff.

General guidance on local housing needs assessment has been published by the former Welsh Office (1999) and by the former Scottish Office (Wood and Preston, 1997). The DETR has recently published good practice guidance on assessing housing needs (DETR 2000d).

General guidance on housing research is published by the Chartered Institute of Housing (Robertson and McLaughlin, 1996), and the Housing Corporation has published specific guidance on assessing black and minority ethnic housing needs (London Research Centre and Lemos and Crane, 1998). There is also advice in the National Housing Federation's (1998) good practice guide *Race Equality in Access to Housing Services*.

Researching the needs of black and minority ethnic communities

A major study of the housing needs of black and minority ethnic communities in **Manchester** was recently published by the Housing Corporation. The research was carried out by staff from the University of Manchester and involved:

- A household survey involving a sample of black and minority ethnic people
- Focus group discussions with people from a variety of black and minority ethnic communities
- Interviews with representatives of black and minority ethnic and mainstream RSLs
- A review of national and local statistical material and studies

The project was assisted by a steering group made up of representatives from RSLs, Manchester City Council, Oldham MBC, the Housing Corporation, the CRE, the National Housing Federation, the University of Manchester and the University of Sheffield (Karn, Mian, Brown and Dale, 1999).

Identifying black and minority ethnic needs

Oxford City Council has commissioned research into good practice in the preparation of black and minority ethnic housing strategies. The study, which includes a service audit, interviews with service users and a community consultation exercise, focuses on two issues: good practice in black and minority ethnic housing strategies generally and services to homeless people. The main outputs are:

- Production of a report to inform the local housing strategy, and a good practice guide on developing local black and minority ethnic housing strategies
- A service audit of housing provision for black and minority ethnic groups, including hostels and day centres, which has identified gaps in provision
- Identification of reasons for the causes of the high incidence of black and minority ethnic groups among the statutory homeless, and the policy implications. The council had become aware of the overrepresentation of black and minority ethnic people through routine ethnic monitoring
- Identification of the causes of low use of supported hostels and day centres among black and minority ethnic groups and the production of a good practice guide for the management of hostels
- Recommendations for improving access to hostels and day centres for single homeless people from the black and minority ethnic communities
- To establish and maintain monitoring of black and minority ethnic households' access to general needs and supported housing

Due to be completed by spring 2001, the project is managed by a multi-agency group which includes housing, social services and the voluntary sector. Progress will be reported regularly to the local housing and community care working group, the housing associations' forum and the Housing Corporation.

A number of factors should be taken into account when gathering information about the needs of black and minority ethnic communities:

- **Sampling**. Simple random sampling for a household survey may not yield enough black and minority ethnic households or, particularly, enough households from some of the smaller communities. It will therefore not be possible to draw conclusions about particular groups, leading to a failure of the strategy to reflect the diversity of the black and minority ethnic communities. To avoid this, there may have to be a boosting of the sample in areas where the particular community(ies) are known to live, in order to maximise the chances of interviewing sufficient numbers of the relevant households. Results must then be weighted when data for the sample as a whole is presented.

- **Hidden needs.** Interviews with heads of households may well fail to uncover the needs of everyone living at a particular address, particularly of people who are staying there temporarily. This problem could be dealt with by training interviewers to be sensitive to the issue and requiring them to seek interviews with the 'hidden' households. Alternatively, the issue may be best approached in a completely different way, for example by gathering information from advice agencies which may have data on homeless people and people in insecure accommodation.

- **Ethnic matching and gender matching of researchers and subjects.** Some people may prefer to talk to someone from the same ethnic background as themselves, particularly if the subject matter of the research is sensitive. Ethnic matching of subject and researcher (interviewer, focus group leader) should therefore be considered. Some women prefer to be interviewed by a woman.

- **Language.** Trained researchers with the appropriate language skills may need to be used

- **Postal surveys.** Problems with response rates and misunderstanding of questions that frequently occur in postal surveys are compounded for people whose first language is not English. Such surveys have a very limited role in research in the field of 'race'.

- **Use of administrative records.** Important opportunities are lost if data is not collected and analysed by ethnic origin. Research based on administrative records should always identify whether black and minority ethnic communities formed part of the research and if so whether their experience differed from that of the indigenous community. Some black and minority ethnic groups are under-represented on waiting lists and in homelessness applications and therefore information on their needs should be collected from a variety of other sources, for example from waiting lists of black and minority ethnic RSLs, from advice agencies and from social surveys.

Using research and data to inform black and minority ethnic housing strategies

Liverpool City Council, in partnership with the Housing Corporation, has adopted a range of research methods to establish a snapshot of the aspirations and expectations of black and minority ethnic people across Merseyside. Merseyside has less than 2% black and minority ethnic population, whilst Liverpool has nearly 4%. The methodology has been designed to reflect this and has taken into account the problem of accessing hidden populations. In Liverpool, an interview schedule will collect information on black and minority ethnic people's views and aspirations of their housing need and opinions on the area in which they live. Local black and minority ethnic people have been recruited and trained to undertake the interviews. However, across Merseyside where there are isolated pockets of black and minority ethnic people, data will be generated by undertaking a range of focus groups organised by identifying black and minority ethnic people across a range of local boroughs.

Manchester City Council has a Geographical Information System (GIS) for mapping the level of demand for its homes. Data from RSLs are being added to this. The Manchester GIS project aims to facilitate the effective assessment, communication and projection of black and minority ethnic housing needs. An interactive atlas of ethnicity in Manchester has been compiled from various data sources and includes the type of stock, its location and condition for all social housing in the city. The atlas also includes employment data and the location of community facilities, for example schools, mosques, shops and health centres.

(Housing Corporation, North West and Merseyside Regional Office, 1999)

■ Identifying the problems and determining intervention strategies

Analysing the issues

Issues and problems arising from consultation and research should be listed and sorted to aid the task of designing solutions. The list should be categorised in terms of the importance attached to issues by consultees and in terms of their degree of complexity. Some could be addressed easily and quickly. Others may require long term solutions or considerable extra resources.

The issues can be categorised in a number of other ways. Some may be amenable to housing solutions; others may require a co-ordinated response from a range of different service providers. Some may require new investment. Others may simply need a change in the rules governing access to existing housing or housing services.

Consideration should be given to the broad shape of the strategy. Intervention under the black and minority ethnic housing strategy must be consistent with the overall housing strategy. However, the housing strategy should not be seen as fixed. It should lay down the broad balance between public and private provision, the overall shape of the authority's investment programme and the role to be played by partner organisations. Over time, work carried out to prepare a black and minority ethnic housing strategy may well identify the need for shifts in priorities, for example for more to be spent on improving private housing or for a wider role for black and minority ethnic RSLs and voluntary organisations. The overall housing strategy may need to be changed to reflect these requirements.

Setting objectives and targets

All strategy documents should set out, in specific terms, what they are seeking to achieve and be linked to an action plan which is regularly reviewed. Black and minority ethnic strategies are no exception to this. Goss and Blackaby (1998) suggest that objectives are set out in a hierarchy with low level specific objectives being linked to high level aims.

A hierarchy of aims and objectives for a black and minority ethnic strategy should span detailed objectives at the lowest level (such as producing monitoring reports on housing allocations), through to intermediate objectives (for example, relating to the equality of opportunity in relation to access to housing). Intermediate objectives should then be linked to the high level aims.

Objectives need to be well grounded and practical. They should be:

- Informed by the consultation process, particularly the views of service users
- Measurable – there is little point in saying that something is to be achieved unless there is a way of measuring whether, and how far, it has been achieved

Objectives and targets can be expressed in a variety of ways. They can relate to **processes**, for example 'all victims of racist harassment will be visited within 48 hours of a complaint being received'. They can relate to **outputs**, for example '20% of homes to be provided by RSLs in the district will be provided by black and minority ethnic RSLs'. Or, they can be **outcome** oriented, for example 'we aim to increase the level of satisfaction of black and minority ethnic tenants by five percentage points over the course of the next year, in order to bring satisfaction levels in line with those of our white tenants'.

Objectives for the achievement of race equality should not be seen as 'specialist' or as 'add ons' to mainstream targets, such as arrears, voids and house improvements. Race targets *are* mainstream. It is simply that they concern outcomes that apply to particular sections of the local population.

Targets set in the black and minority ethnic housing strategy should be fully integrated into Best Value arrangements. Government guidance emphasises the need to address equity considerations in Best Value reviews. Guidance contained in DETR Circular 10/99 states that reviews should consider ways in which services have an impact on all sections of the community, including minority groups. Targets should be set to redress disparities in the provision of services to those who are disadvantaged (DETR, 1999a).

Reports on key outcomes could also be published alongside other indicators in authorities' performance reports to tenants and other citizens. Many authorities set personal performance targets for chief and senior officers. These should include some of the key targets from the black and minority ethnic strategy.

■ Option appraisal

Identifying the options for meeting the needs of black and minority ethnic communities should be an inclusive process involving representatives of the communities concerned. Options cannot be confined to provision by the authority, although directly provided services will often have an important role to play.

There will be a variety of ways in which RSLs and other agencies, such as community and voluntary organisations, private companies and statutory agencies, can be involved in implementing the strategy.

Examples of options that may need to be evaluated

Options for new provision targeted at black and minority ethnic communities:
- New build
- Acquisition and/or improvement of existing dwellings
- Conversion of existing dwellings

Groups that could be involved in these programmes:
- The authority itself
- White-led RSLs
- Black and minority ethnic RSLs
- Private builders
- The local community

Options for co-ordinating the response to racist harassment:
- Improving existing interagency procedures
- Setting up new community-based anti harassment projects

Options for advice and information to black and minority ethnic communities:
- Local authority advice centres
- Funding voluntary organisations to provide advice services
- Local authority outreach workers seconded to community organisations

Further guidance about option appraisal, including criteria for evaluating options, can be found within the CIH/LGA Good Practice Guide on housing strategies (Goss and Blackaby, 1998).

■ Implementation

The implementation of a black and minority ethnic strategy requires an action plan to achieve necessary change. Without such a plan, it is difficult to see how broad strategies can be turned into effective measures to tackle discrimination and disadvantage. In a study of English RSLs' approaches to meeting black and minority ethnic needs, Tomlins et al (2000) found that only 21% of RSLs with a written race equality policy had an action plan to implement it.

Action plans should include a list of desired outcomes, each of which identifies responsibilities and resources, a timetable and a procedure for review.

Implementing the black and minority ethnic housing strategy

Bradford MDC has established a Race and Housing Executive Group to oversee the implementation of policies aimed at meeting the housing needs of black and minority ethnic communities. The Executive comprises the council's Chair and Director of Housing and Chair of the Equal Rights Sub-committee, the Regional Director of the Housing Corporation, the Director of Bradford Racial Equality Council and a local academic.

The Executive Group will monitor and help move forward race and housing targets included in the 1999/2001 joint housing strategy produced by the multi-agency Bradford Housing Forum. Some of these targets are:

- The anti-racial harassment initiative, which has recently been expanded to cover the whole district
- The development and implementation of inner area renewal zones to improve inner city areas suffering decline
- The completion of a survey on access to social housing by the currently under-represented Asian communities
- The completion of research into the housing needs of African and Caribbean communities
- Training of council and RSL staff in equal opportunities and cultural awareness
- Supporting Manningham Housing Association's research into black and Asian women's support and accommodation needs where they are fleeing violence, and supporting the building of a black and Asian women's refuge, together with a network of safe homes

The allocation of responsibilities to named individuals is important. This may be achieved through appointing a lead officer who negotiates with other officers the implementation of specific tasks. Target setting needs to be done in consultation with all those concerned and timescales should be realistic.

There may need to be a programme of training for employees on ethnic diversity and disadvantage or training to help them to carry out some of the tasks in the action plan. Training may also be required on new procedures or methods of consultation.

The financial implications of the strategy will need to be considered. Some aspects of the strategy may require additional resources before they can be delivered. This may involve capital resources, revenue funding for particular services, grant aid to outside organisations or changes to existing budgets, such as the training budget.

■ Monitoring and evaluation

It is important to consider early on how the strategy will be monitored and evaluated. Asking the question: 'how will we know whether the strategy has been a success?' will help to define specific race equality outcomes that are desired. It is also important to consider the role to be played by the black and minority ethnic communities and other stakeholders in evaluation, and whether an independent evaluation should be conducted at some stage.

Further guidance on monitoring and evaluation can be found in chapter 7.

❏ Content of black and minority ethnic housing strategies

The precise content of a black and minority ethnic strategy will vary according to local circumstances. Strategies should, however, take full account of:

- Statutory and regulatory responsibilities
- The outcome of consultation exercises
- Local research findings

Black and minority ethnic housing strategies

In 1998, **Rochdale MBC** and **Ashiana Housing Association**, a black and minority ethnic RSL, launched a major housing strategy for the Asian communities in the area. The strategy followed consultation with 39 organisations, including welfare and community organisations working with Asian communities and local mosques.

The overall aim of the strategy is to eliminate housing and related disadvantage in Rochdale's Asian communities by the time of the 2011 census. The strategy sets out policies and initiatives in the following areas:

- Housing and renewing inner Rochdale
- Access to social housing
- Housing and community care needs
- The housing needs of young Asians

The strategy is being implemented by the council in partnership with a number of other organisations, including Ashiana Housing Association. A number of priorities for action have been identified, including:

- Building new homes on available sites
- Establishing an improvement agency
- Setting up a housing co-operative
- Grants for home extensions to tackle overcrowding
- Establishing a multi-agency racist harassment forum
- Establishing an out of hours racist harassment emergency service
- Employing more bi-lingual staff
- Setting targets to increase the proportion of black and minority ethnic staff to reflect the projected 14% black and minority ethnic community in Rochdale by 2011
- Promoting sheltered housing amongst the Asian communities
- Housing and employment initiatives targeted at young people

The strategy document includes a detailed action plan that sets out the objective to be achieved on an annual basis, how this will be measured in terms of outputs, the target month or year for completion and who is taking the lead.

It is important that strategies reflect the full range of needs felt by black and minority ethnic communities and are not just confined to needs that can be met, on one hand, through local authorities' roles as landlords or, on the other, through 'specialist' agencies, such as black and minority ethnic RSLs. In particular strategies should:

- Address race equality issues in all social housing in the district

- Consider ways in which needs can be met in the private sector
- Deal with race equality in 'day to day' services such as housing management, maintenance and improvement services. The Commission for Racial Equality *Race Relations Code of Practice in Rented Housing* (quoted in the report of Policy Action Team 5 on Housing Management) provides useful guidance for housing managers
- Propose ways in which black and minority ethnic communities can be empowered
- Reflect the wider corporate agenda

Achieving the CRE's standards

Sandwell MBC has made a formal commitment to achieving the CRE's standard for race equality as set out in the Commission's publication *Racial Equality Means Quality* (1996). It aims to reach the highest level of the standard (level 5) by late 2000 and then to seek continuous improvements thereafter. The initiative involves all council services.

In the housing service, the project is being carried out by an implementation group of senior officers which meets monthly and is monitored by the housing service group. A detailed resource pack has been produced for all managers which provides information on the initiative. All managers have attended a one-day training course and have, in turn, briefed their staff on what is expected of them. Training is also being provided for caretakers and concierges.

Action plans setting out tasks that need to be completed are being produced for each division and team within the service. The action plan describes:

- Action/target to be achieved by divisions
- Each level within the CRE's standard which is addressed by an action
- What evidence exists to verify that the standard has been met
- Whether the evidence is adequate to meet the standard set
- If it is not adequate, what needs to be done to ensure it does meet the standard, who is to take the necessary action and by when

A suggested way to structure a black and minority ethnic housing strategy is set out below:

Black and minority ethnic housing strategy: an outline

- Aims

- How the strategy was drawn up:
  - Consultation
  - Information gathering
  - Option appraisal

- Ways in which black and minority ethnic needs are to be met:
  - New investment
  - New services
  - Changes in existing services

- Policies to ensure race equality in:
  - Services
  - Employment
  - Opportunities for involvement

- Tackling racist harassment

- Links to other strategies:
  - Community regeneration
  - Community safety
  - Community care
  - Anti-poverty
  - Older people
  - Young people

- How the strategy is to be implemented:
  - Action by the authority
  - Action by other organisations

- Action plan

- Monitoring and review arrangements

Black and minority ethnic housing strategies

Although Gosport has relatively few people from black and minority ethnic communities (about 1%), **Gosport BC** has decided to prepare a minority ethnic housing strategy and has consulted local organisations on a draft document. The strategy, published in June 2000, contains a number of objectives, including:

- Continued ethnic monitoring of the joint housing register and the introduction of ethnic monitoring of private sector grant applications and of formal complaints
- Staff training in equal opportunity issues
- Continued use of a language line service which provides a telephone based simultaneous interpreting service
- Introduction of policy and procedures to tackle racial harassment
- Working with RSLs to monitor access to housing, and racial harassment

Gloucester City Council's Black and Minority Ethnic Housing Strategy, which is summarised within its housing strategy statement, includes specific targets to be achieved in the forthcoming year. The targets include items that are ongoing from year to year, such as support for the black community through capacity building with community groups, and training and employment schemes as part of the SRB programme, and also new key tasks, for example an evaluation of young black and minority ethnic people's housing needs. Each year's housing strategy statement includes a statement of progress on the targets set the previous year. The statement includes both things that have gone well and work which has not progressed as quickly as had been hoped.

Key questions

- *Has your organisation got a written black and minority ethnic strategy?*
- *If so, has it been reviewed recently?*
- *If not, is there a commitment to produce one?*
- *Where it is intended to produce a new strategy, are effective processes (based on the guidance outlined in this chapter) in place?*

CHAPTER 3

AIMING FOR RACE EQUALITY: THE FRAMEWORK

This chapter discusses:
- Communication
- Involving black and minority ethnic communities in designing strategies and services
- Employment and training

❏ Communication

Black and minority communities can face disadvantage if housing organisations fail to communicate properly, or if the communities are not given adequate opportunities to communicate with the organisation from which they require services. Organisations should have a range of mechanisms in place to enable the community to be involved in important decisions about their housing and related issues. This may include overcoming issues of language especially where English may not be the first language spoken. However, it is also about:

- Putting mechanisms in place which allow an honest and open dialogue between the organisation and the community
- Recognising that location, time, access, transport and childcare will affect whether particular groups are likely to participate. Specifically, there might be a need for separate mechanisms provided by black and minority ethnic women for black and minority ethnic women who may not engage effectively in open forums.

■ Written communication

Organisations providing housing services should develop clear policies about their communication with black and minority ethnic communities. It is important to review the full range of written information provided to service users and potential service users, such as reports, leaflets and standard letters. The languages into which material should be translated will vary from area to area. Before making decisions about which languages should be used, housing organisations should consult with local community organisations serving or representing the various black and minority ethnic communities. There may also be local social survey data which indicates which are the main languages spoken in the area.

The most important documents will need to be fully translated into the appropriate languages. For the remaining documents, organisations can reasonably adopt a 'translate or explain on request' approach. This means a translated statement prominently displayed on each document which says briefly what the document is about and what people should do if they want a translation, or (where possible) an oral explanation of what it says, in the appropriate language. Some housing organisations in Scotland are developing proposals to have a 'happy to translate' logo on letters and other documents (see page 81).

A named member of staff should have responsibility for regularly reviewing and updating all written information in accordance with a set timetable.

Survey results

Communication

- 28% of authorities have taken specific action to promote their housing services to black and minority ethnic communities. In areas where the minority ethnic population is 10% or more of the total, 78% of authorities have taken specific action. The most frequently cited methods for communication are: leaflets, posters, working through black and minority ethnic organisations and specialist outreach workers.

- 44% of authorities said they provide leaflets, audio tapes or videos in different languages. However, some of these did not provide translated leaflets as a matter of routine – only if requested. 91% of authorities in areas where the black and minority population is 10% or more provide translated material. The topics most frequently covered in translated material are: housing allocations, racist harassment policies and procedures, complaints procedures and improvement grants.

- 81% of authorities said they make arrangements to assist service users/potential service users who do not speak English, such as by employing interpreters, or using existing staff who can speak other languages. All authorities where the black and minority ethnic population is 10% or more make such arrangements. Mostly, interpreting services are brought in from outside agencies.

Organisations should make sure that inclusive images of the community are shown on all literature they produce. Leaflets showing only white service users may suggest that the services are not appropriate for people from black and minority ethnic communities.

■ Oral communication

There are several ways for an organisation to ensure that it provides adequate interpreting and translation services. One option, as part of a more general strategy to boost the availability of interpreters, is to recognise community languages as a recognised skill which appears in job descriptions as appropriate and is properly rewarded, for example by an extra increment. Employing more front line staff, such as housing officers, with the appropriate language skills will undoubtedly improve communication with service users whose first language is not English. It enables service users to communicate directly with someone with housing expertise. It is recognised, however, that this will not always be possible and organisations may also need to consider the following options:

- Directly employed interpreters. In the case of local authorities, these might be a resource that is shared between departments
- Use of outside interpreting agencies
- Use of telephone services, such as Language Line
- Jointly establishing an interpreting service to be shared between the local authority, RSLs and other service providers

Organisations should avoid giving interpreting work to staff who have no formal responsibilities for it but who simply happen to have the appropriate language skills. Staff who are constantly called away from their proper duties to do interpreting will become frustrated. Where it is to be provided in-house, interpreting should be carried out by staff who have this responsibility written into their job descriptions.

Organisations should be sensitive to the fact that some women will want to have a female interpreter.

■ Other methods of communication

There are a number of other ways of communicating with those needing or using housing services:

- Audio tapes. There are, for example, tapes explaining sheltered housing in a variety of languages

- Videos
- Local radio
- Open days
- Exhibitions
- Seminars and conferences

Organisations need to make sure that information is provided in a way that is accessible to people with sensory disabilities.

■ Supporting community resources

Some people from black and minority ethnic communities may not approach housing organisations for help and information because they mistrust 'officials', or because they may have had bad experiences in the past. They may turn to sources of help within their own community – to community representatives, voluntary advice agencies, temples, mosques or black churches. Recognising this, housing organisations should consider the following means of supporting information sources within the community:

- Providing community organisations with training and resource packs on housing services and options
- Funding voluntary advice agencies working with black and minority ethnic communities
- Seconding 'outreach' staff to work with community organisations; for example, staff could provide regular advice sessions at community organisations' premises
- Working with black and minority ethnic RSLs which have access to particular communities

❑ Involving black and minority ethnic communities in designing strategies and services

Community involvement is a vital component of Best Value arrangements. Government guidance stresses the importance of involving, in Best Value reviews, service users and potential service users who have traditionally been under-represented (DETR, 1999a).

Effective involvement of black and minority ethnic people brings about a number of benefits:

- Improved services which better reflect the needs of all service users
- Improved community spirit
- Harnessing of community resources to tackle racism
- Improving the sense of 'ownership' amongst all residents in an area, leading to lower tenancy turnover and decreased levels of vandalism

It is important that, reflecting their range of functions, local authorities have strategies to consult with all categories of service users and potential service users. If all efforts are directed at involving tenants, other service user groups will lose out. The groups not included may have disproportionate numbers of black and minority ethnic people, for example applicants for housing and renovation grant applicants. Confining involvement to council tenants and not also giving a say to owner occupiers or homeless people may lead to a biased view about capital spending or housing allocation priorities.

■ Maximising the opportunities for involvement

The key to inclusive service user involvement is providing a number of opportunities for people to participate. Having a variety of involvement methods means that individual service users can choose which ones suit them best. According to the DETR's good practice guide on tenant participation (Cole, Hickman, Millward and Reid, 1999), there are four broad types of involvement methods:

- Individually, for example through surveys
- Through representative individuals, for example through focus groups
- Collectively, for example at public meetings
- Through representative collectives, for example tenants' associations

Specific approaches to involvement of black and minority ethnic communities include:

- **Focus groups** – specific groups of local people can be brought together to discuss a particular issue in some depth and establish their opinions. Focus groups can accommodate the diversity and differing cultural expectations of certain groups because discussions can be organised to take account of gender, age and ethnicity.
- **Recruiting ethnic-specific community development workers/link workers** – such workers can help to bridge the divide between organisations and the local communities.

- **Neighbourhood conferences** – these can be a useful tool in bringing together local people and professionals. Black and minority ethnic people should be involved in organising the event and encouraging local people to attend.

- **Community surveys** – local black and minority ethnic people can be recruited to carry out research within their own communities.

- **Local forums** – a local black and minority ethnic forum may focus specifically on housing or have a broader remit. These forums can establish two-way communication with other agencies.

- **Citizens' juries** – a group of citizens is selected through a random process and invited to work together for a number of days on exploring a problem, hearing expert evidence and making recommendations.

- **Residential events** – these could be aimed at particular groups, for example young people.

- **Use of local media** – in some areas, local radio stations have time slots aimed at particular communities. There are also local newspapers which are aimed at particular communities. These can be accessed to advertise a range of activities and generate interest.

Community capacity building

Research in the **London Borough of Camden** has shown that Bangladeshi residents are less likely than other groups to belong to tenants' associations and many are unaware of what a tenants' association does. To address this, the Housing Department and the Equalities Unit worked with Hopscotch and the Camden Federation of Tenants to produce a video *How to Improve Your Housing Situation – What Can Tenants' Associations Do For You?*

The video, in Sylheti and English, aims to encourage Bangladeshi tenants to get involved in their association by explaining their role, giving examples of how they worked successfully and addressing possible obstacles to participating, for example language problems or fear of racism. The housing department has trained a number of the Bangladeshi women project workers involved in the capacity building exercise and has worked with them and local tenants' association representatives to publicise the video and arrange special screenings.

■ How far consultative mechanisms are representative

Housing organisations should address the extent to which tenants' and residents' associations, and the forums that are based on them, are representative. The National Housing Federation guide *Race Equality in Access to Housing Services* (1998) states that there are three elements of representativeness:

- Whether black and minority ethnic people are involved in the organisations
- Whether black and minority ethnic people are heard and their views given equal weight
- Whether black and minority ethnic people have the opportunity to hold official positions in organisations and to represent the organisations at public occasions

The research carried out by Cole, Hickman, Millward and Reid (1999) found that some local authorities have developed ways of involving groups who are often excluded from participation structures. These methods fall into four main categories:

- Through developing separate participatory structures for black and minority ethnic communities
- By taking participation out of council offices to the excluded groups
- By being aware of the needs of excluded groups and providing for them
- By making sure mainstream participation structures do not discriminate

It is important that, where separate participatory structures are set up, they are not marginalised in that people's role is limited to discussing 'race' issues. One way of reducing this risk is to have arrangements in which representatives from the black and minority ethnic consultative forum sit on mainstream groups, such as the district-wide tenants' council, or groups discussing Best Value, housing allocations, repairs and so on.

Separate consultative structures may only be a temporary measure. They allow people to gain confidence and to see the benefits of involvement, but after a while it may be appropriate to merge separate forums with mainstream consultative arrangements.

Efforts to ensure that mainstream consultative arrangements do not discriminate can include:

- Making the existence of effective equal opportunities policies and practices a prerequisite for recognition and funding of residents' and tenants' associations

- Monitoring the ethnicity of residents' and tenants' association committees
- Providing anti-discrimination training for community representatives

'Recognition criteria' can include some or all of the following:

- A commitment to equal opportunities in general, and race equality in particular, in the constitution or other written documents
- An expectation that policies will be enforced, and that action will be taken against any breaches
- An agreement that meetings will be conducted in a way that encourages the involvement of black and minority ethnic people
- Acceptance of targets for increasing the involvement of black and minority ethnic people

Survey results

Consultation with tenants and housing applicants

Excluding stock transfer authorities, 15% of authorities have specific mechanisms to consult with black and minority ethnic tenants and applicants. Of authorities where the black and minority ethnic population made up 10% or more of the total, the percentage with specific mechanisms was 43%. Consultative forums and consultation via letter are the most frequently used methods.

Regarding consultative arrangements generally, 18% of non stock transfer authorities have mechanisms to check whether consultative structures have adequate representation of black and minority ethnic tenants. Of authorities where the black and minority ethnic population makes up 10% or more of the total, 43% have such mechanisms.

Of all authorities where there were tenants' or residents' associations covering their housing areas (stock transfer authorities were excluded), 88% of authorities say they expect the associations to comply with race equality policies.

31% of non-stock transfer authorities have, in the last five years, provided or arranged training in race equality issues for tenants' or residents' representatives.

90% of authorities, where the black and minority ethnic population is 10% or more of the total, have provided or arranged training.

■ Tenant Compacts

The introduction of Tenant Compacts provides an excellent opportunity to review current approaches to the involvement of council tenants in issues of housing management. All local authority landlords in England and Wales are expected to sign agreements with their tenants on how tenants are involved in decisions about their homes. The Scottish Executive is planning to introduce a statutory right to participation for tenants in Scotland. The right would extend both to individual tenants through their tenancy agreements and to recognised tenants' groups.

The DETR's framework document for the compacts (DETR, 1999d) states that local authorities should draw up equality strategies, negotiated with tenants, which seek to involve black and minority ethnic tenants where they are under-represented. The framework document goes on to say that equality objectives could be established which set standards for consultation and which monitor levels of involvement and representation by all groups, including ethnic minorities.

Consultation with black and minority ethnic communities

In the **London Borough of Southwark**, the Black and Minority Ethnic Tenants' and Residents' Organisation (SBMETRO) was formed in 1995 with support from the Housing Community Development Section and the Southwark Group of Tenant Organisations (SGTO). The organisation acts as a voice for black and minority ethnic tenants and residents and supports them in their efforts to become involved in tenants' and residents' associations. It works with associations to encourage higher levels of participation from black and minority ethnic people.

SBMETRO nominates representatives to be full members of Neighbourhood Forums and the borough-wide Tenant Council. The organisation has recently moved into its own office and has received funding from the council's Tenant Fund. It is currently developing a more extensive funding application to go to the Tenant Fund Management Committee, seeking resources to appoint a project officer.

The SGTO has received additional funding in 1999/2000 from the Tenant Fund to appoint a development worker to work with tenants' and residents' associations. The aim is to support and encourage these associations to develop good practice in terms of seeking greater representation from the black and minority ethnic communities.

For recognition purposes, all tenants' and residents' associations have to adopt a standard constitution that reflects the CRE's recommendations on good practice. The constitution should include the following clauses:

- To promote the harmonious functioning of a multi-racial community and to work towards the elimination of all forms of racism and discrimination within it
- The composition of the committee shall, as far as possible, represent the multi-racial character of the estate

Neighbourhood Forums and the Tenant Council have membership clauses that give places to under-represented sections of the community, including black and minority ethnic delegates.

Manchester City Council Housing Department has developed an extensive consultation programme by setting up a community consultative forum (CCF), involving black and other minority ethnic community representatives. The aim is to improve housing provision and service delivery, eliminate racism in employment and empower black and minority ethnic communities to participate in the decision-making process. The CCF meets on a quarterly basis.

Among the issues discussed at the forum are:

- Implementation of the Race Equality Strategy
- Best Value
- A review of estate management
- The council's crime and disorder strategy
- Findings from Housing Corporation funded research on the housing needs of black and minority ethnic communities in Manchester
- A review of racial harassment policy and procedures
- Ethnic record keeping and monitoring
- Positive Action Training Scheme
- Equal opportunity in recruitment and selection

At the request of the forum, the housing department has developed a housing awareness training programme for volunteers from the black and minority ethnic communities. The aim is to equip the volunteers with sufficient knowledge to enable them to deal with queries from community members. The training covers issues such as homelessness, repairs, rehousing and tackling neighbour nuisance.

■ The practicalities of involvement

Attention to the detail of community involvement is crucial. Getting the practicalities right involves being sensitive to different needs and preferences:

- Some women may not participate in discussions in a large public meeting, particularly when men are present, but they may make a lively contribution in a meeting for women only, particularly where the discussion is led by a woman who understands their culture and can speak in the participants' first language

- Parents may find it difficult to attend an event unless there are childcare arrangements

- It is important to choose an appropriate place for meetings. Some people may not attend a meeting at the town hall, but would participate fully in a meeting held at a local community centre, school or place of worship

- Interpreters may need to be available

- Publicity material needs to be devised in a way that will encourage black and minority ethnic people to attend

- Meetings should be conducted in a way that encourages everyone to participate

- Black and minority ethnic people may need to be supported during the meeting

- There is a need to make sure that some meetings focus on the specific concerns of black and minority ethnic communities

- Social activities should be planned to ensure that they can be enjoyed by all

- Discriminatory comments or racist language must not be tolerated

It is a case of thinking through the best approach – often there is a need to consult on a small scale about how a more wide-ranging exercise should be undertaken. It is important to learn from past experience – success should be built on and failures should lead to learning for next time

There is not enough space in this Guide to discuss all of the issues about involvement. There are several useful guides giving practical advice about the involvement of black and minority ethnic people, for example: CRE (1993), Tenants' Participation Advisory Service (England) (1993), Clark (1994), Tenants' Participation Advisory Service (England) (1994) and Jeffrey and Seager (1995).

Community involvement: what should be monitored

✔ Profile of ethnic origin of people participating in consultative activities: meetings, surveys, panels etc compared with profile of the communities as a whole, or service users

✔ Comparison of participation rates by the different ethnic groups between various consultative methods employed

✔ Ethnic origin profile of residents' and tenants' association committees

✔ Comparisons between the various ethnic groups of views about the way they are being involved

Tenant participation

The Northmoor Road Initiative has been set up in the Longsight area of Manchester. The aim of this project, led by **Manchester Methodist Housing Association** in partnership with **Manchester City Council**, is to build on existing community structures within the Northmoor Road area in order to foster the active involvement of black and minority ethnic groups. A full time community link worker has been employed to facilitate the contribution of black and minority ethnic groups to the physical, social and economic programmes within the area.

The project aims to develop good practice through the investigation and development of traditional methods of participation, which are often seen as barriers to the involvement of black and minority ethnic groups. It will also aim to develop an effective strategy to ensure the continued involvement of all sections of the community within the Northmoor Road area.

(Housing Corporation, North West and Merseyside Regional Office, 1999)

❑ Employment and training

No organisation will be able to incorporate race equality principles fully into its services unless it has a diverse workforce that is committed to equality aims and that understands how discrimination occurs and how it can be avoided. An organisation will fail to provide culturally competent services unless its organisational structure is inclusive and diverse, and an organisation that is not demonstrably committed to equality of opportunity in its employment policy and practices will not be able to convince anyone, particularly people from black and minority ethnic communities, that it is seriously trying to provide services that are fair and sensitive to different needs. Housing organisations therefore need to be equally committed to race equality in both employment and service delivery.

Many housing organisations have adopted an aim of having a workforce whose ethnic profile, at all levels, matches in broad terms the profile of the people in the district it is seeking to serve. This aim provides the focus for recruitment and other employment policies and guides the organisation in its efforts to promote diversity in the workplace. There is a strong business case for this approach: an organisation recruiting and retaining talent from all sections of the working population is more likely to have an efficient and effective workforce. The Housing Corporation has recently embarked on a project to promote diversity in the workplace, beginning with an examination of its own employment practice and culture.

Race equality in employment policies and practices covers a broad range of issues. Policies need to cover fair recruitment and career progression, and must seek to understand why staff leave or feel dissatisfied, and address problems where they exist. They should also embrace the culture and working environment, including the way in which harassment is to be dealt with and how employees are to be supported and trained.

For personnel teams to have a true commitment to the agreed targets around recruitment and retention of black and minority ethnic staff, it is important that they are fully involved in the black and minority ethnic housing strategy from the earliest stages, and incorporate the objectives in their own performance targets and action plans.

■ Equality standards

Guidance on the legal framework for race equality in employment is contained in the CRE's Race Relations Code of Practice in Employment (1984). The Commission has also published a report setting out standards for race equality aimed at employers (Commission for Racial Equality, 1995a). This standard seeks to help organisations to assess their current position, to consider the range of action they can take to achieve change and to measure progress. It sets out a wide range of standards, arranged under five levels, in the following areas of activity:

- Policy and planning
- Recruitment, promotion, training, dismissal and redundancy
- Developing and retaining staff
- Communication and corporate image
- Corporate citizenship
- Auditing for race equality

Fair recruitment and selection

Manchester City Council has published a simple 11 page booklet that summarises its policies on equal opportunities in employment. The guide describes the scope of the policy, how to complain if there is a breach of the policy and who is responsible for making the policy work. The guide is available on request in Punjabi, Gujerati, Bengali, Urdu and Chinese, as well as on tape and in Braille.

Specific advice to local authorities is contained within the Commission's standards for local government. There are separate documents for Scotland (Commission for Racial Equality, 1995b) and for England and Wales (Commission for Racial Equality, 1996). One area of the standards concerns recruitment, selection and staff development and retention. Again standards are set at different levels with the intention that authorities will progress through the levels.

Increasing the number of black and minority ethnic managers

Bradford MDC has launched a Black People into Management initiative which seeks to address the under-representation of black and minority ethnic employees at senior levels within the authority.

The initiative involves:

- Press advertising in ethnic and regional media which is particularly aimed at black and minority ethnic parents so that they can encourage their sons and daughters to apply for jobs

- A promotional video highlighting the range of professional career opportunities that are available
- Consultation with existing black and minority ethnic staff to identify areas where improvements in employment and management practice may be needed
- A fast track development scheme for black and minority ethnic employees. This currently contains six places but will be expanded to 20 places
- A positive action training scheme
- A mentoring scheme for black and minority ethnic employees
- Opportunities for black and minority ethnic staff to undertake work shadowing and secondments in other departments
- Ethnic minorities represented on selection and interview panels wherever possible at all stages of the recruitment process
- Leaver questionnaires and interviews

The results of the initiative are being monitored closely both by chief officers and by senior councillors.

■ Specialist staff

Responsibility for ensuring race equality in service delivery rests with all employees. However, there may be a need for housing organisations to consider appointing specialist staff to help with particular aspects of service delivery, or to help set the policy and monitoring frameworks.

Specialist staff can perform a variety of different roles:
- Policy development
- Monitoring
- Consultation and participation
- Providing services to particular communities
- Outreach work
- Supporting victims of racist harassment
- Translating and interpreting

Career development for black and minority ethnic employees

Birmingham City Council has carried out a comprehensive review of its Breaking Through initiative which aims to look at the position of its employees from black and minority ethnic communities. It has now launched a corporate initiative, known as Bridges into the Future, which seeks to tackle problems identified in the course of the review. The initiative aims to make sure that equal opportunities in employment are fully translated into practice, that there is a career development planning process for all staff and that black and minority ethnic staff receive more support.

Each department of the council has been asked to produce an implementation strategy in order to make sure that Breaking Through objectives are met. Among the action points included in the housing department's strategy are:

- Introducing a mentoring scheme for black and minority ethnic employees

- Setting up a system for auditing the employee selection process

- Producing guidelines for maximising learning and development opportunities through such measures as project teams, secondments and 'acting up'

- Widening access to training by publishing a list of 'approved' qualifications and reviewing procedures for accessing courses, including using criteria that prioritise under-represented groups and employees without formal qualifications

The council also has reserved places for black and minority ethnic staff on its management development programme, training schemes and student placements.

It is vitally important that specialist staff are not marginalised or isolated and do not feel that they are being asked to carry the whole responsibility for race equality within the organisation. These problems can be avoided if:

- Senior management demonstrates a full commitment to meeting its responsibilities on race equality and 'leads from the front' on 'race' issues

51

- Race equality issues are fully integrated into all policies and procedures and employees receive clear guidance and training on what is expected of them

- The specialist staff are themselves adequately supported by their managers and have access to administrative, IT and training resources

- Specialist staff are encouraged to form networks with other people in similar positions

■ Training

Race equality training

An appropriately trained workforce is essential to the delivery of services that embody race equality principles. Employees need to understand the law relating to 'race', how discrimination occurs, including how their own actions at work can disadvantage particular groups of people and what are the organisation's policies to combat unlawful discrimination. Crucial to this last topic is an understanding of what each team and individual needs to do to promote the organisation's equality objectives.

Priority groups for race equality training are:

- The housing committee or board of management

- Senior managers

- Staff involved in recruitment

- Team leaders

- All employees who use discretion in their work

By itself training is not sufficient and will only be successful if it is backed up by equality policies and procedures and commitment from the top management in the organisation. The CRE's curriculum guide on race equality training (1991a) says that training will not be successful unless there is:

- Senior management support for the training. Those at the top must be seen to be part of the training process

- Continuing management support for the training effort

- Back-up for any subsequent changes in practices and policies

- Careful consideration of the resources needed

Survey results

Percentage of authorities where employees have received training in race equality issues

	All or most employees	Some employees	Total
Senior managers	36%	20%	56%
Middle managers	36%	22%	58%
Front line	34%	18%	52%
Estate based	26%	14%	40%
Wardens/care staff	15%	19%	34%
Technical	18%	20%	38%
Support/admin	21%	16%	37%
Manual	11%	12%	23%

 22% of authorities have, in the last five years, run training schemes designed to help people from under-represented racial groups, for example, PATH or similar schemes

Positive action

One way of addressing the under-representation of black and minority ethnic people in an organisation's work force is through the use of the positive action provisions in the Race Relations Act 1976 regarding training. These provisions apply to training existing employees and to promoting access to training for those who are not currently employed and who are members of a racial group that is under-represented.

Positive action in training

Sandwell MBC has run a Positive Action Training in Housing (PATH) scheme for 10 years. Four trainees are taken on each year.
The period of training is one year for housing management and two years for technical roles. There is no guarantee about subsequent employment but, over the 10 years, 80% of trainees have secured permanent employment after completion of the training programme.

The PATH Local Authorities scheme provides a successful model to train black and minority ethnic people to become housing managers in local authority housing departments and RSLs. It was established in 1987. In its tenth anniversary report, PATH LA announced that, in ten years, almost 300 people had been trained. Of these, 91% had obtained jobs on or before completion of the training course and, of these, 85% obtained jobs at senior officer or principal officer grade (PATH LA, 1997).

While PATH schemes can achieve a great deal in supporting the career development of black and minority ethnic staff, wider changes are still needed, since the problem remains that designated schemes can underestimate the potential of black and minority ethnic staff by implying that they need special help to progress.

Employment and training: what should be monitored

✔ Comparisons between the ethnic origin profile of those applying, being shortlisted and being offered jobs

✔ Analysis of ethnic origin of those who are promoted or re-graded

✔ Analysis of ethnic origin of current employees at the various grades/levels and time spent at each grade

✔ Comparison between the ethnic origin profile of those receiving training and the profile of the workforce as a whole

✔ Analysis of the ethnic origin profile of those against whom disciplinary action is taken compared with the profile of the workforce as a whole

✔ Analysis of ethnic origin profile of those leaving the organisation and reasons for leaving

Key questions

- *Have approaches to communication and consultation been reviewed recently?*

- *Have black and minority ethnic people been asked what they think about the way the organisation communicates and consults with them?*

- *Have opportunities been taken in Best Value reviews and in Tenant Compacts to critically review current approaches to involving black and minority ethnic communities?*

- *Does the organisation comply with the CRE's Code of Practice in Employment?*

- *Is the organisation committed to meeting the CRE's standards for local government?*

CHAPTER 4

AIMING FOR RACE EQUALITY: THE STRATEGIC ROLE AND SERVICES TO THE WIDER COMMUNITY

This chapter discusses:
- Providing housing
- Community regeneration
- Improving conditions in private sector housing
- Services to homeless people
- Housing advice and information
- Services for people with care and support needs
- Services for refugees and asylum seekers

❑ Providing housing

The importance of the proper assessment of need, and consultation about new provision, cannot be overstated. Housing is an expensive commodity and is expected to last a long time. Bad design or poor location may mean that housing intended for particular communities proves to be unsuitable, and mistakes made at the planning stage may be impossible to put right.

Providing social housing, whether by new build or by acquisition, often involves a number of agencies:

- Local authorities are involved in setting the strategic framework, in analysing information about local needs, in setting priorities and in some cases providing land
- RSLs may be involved in providing the homes and in managing them subsequently

- The Housing Corporation/Scottish Homes/National Assembly for Wales are often involved in providing the funding
- Community organisations have a role in advising on needs and may also be involved in publicising the completed schemes

Housing provision which properly meets the needs of black and minority ethnic groups requires effective joint working between these agencies. Local authorities play an important part in bringing the agencies together.

■ Location

People's preferences to live in certain areas are shaped by several factors, including access to work, schools and community facilities and proximity to relatives and friends. Black and minority ethnic people's choices about where they live may be more constrained than those of white people because:

- They may not be so fully aware of what housing is available in different areas
- Many may want to live in areas they already know and where there are community networks and services, and will reject other areas which have a history of racist harassment
- Many have lower than average incomes and will not be able to afford many of the homes that could potentially be available

Housing providers often face the problem that, in traditional areas of settlement by black and minority ethnic communities, the opportunities for new provision are limited because of shortages of housing land. A further problem is that areas of traditional settlement are often amongst the most deprived within a district and there is therefore a danger that, by concentrating new provision in these areas, it simply reinforces existing patterns of deprivation.

Survey results

Meeting the needs of black and minority ethnic people

22% of authorities have policies that seek to ensure that new or refurbished housing addresses the needs of black and minority ethnic people. In most cases, appropriate provision was said to be achieved by working with black and minority ethnic RSLs.

Strategies to provide homes targeted at black and minority ethnic communities need to be based on an understanding of needs and of these kinds of constraints. Depending on the circumstances in each area, local authorities should thoroughly explore, in consultation with local communities, the scope both for meeting needs within traditional areas of settlement, as well as in other areas – areas perhaps accessible by public transport from traditional settlement areas. The strategy may need to involve:

- Provision in traditional areas with an emphasis on exploiting all available opportunities, including rehabilitation of existing homes, purchase of existing satisfactory dwellings or management of existing dwellings. Local authorities may need to use their land assembly powers to facilitate the development of complex sites. 'Housing plus' activities may well be particularly appropriate as part of comprehensive regeneration approaches in these areas

- Appropriate provision in other areas involving close partnerships with community organisations. Having identified areas that are accessible and which do not have a history of racist harassment, the strategy would need to involve, not only appropriate housing, but also good communication with the relevant communities and support to the new tenants, who may otherwise feel isolated. Effective implementation of policies to tackle racist harassment is also essential.

Provision by black and minority ethnic RSLs can be particularly appropriate to the strategy because they may help black and minority ethnic people to gain confidence to live in areas which, previously, they would not have considered. There is further discussion about the role of black and minority ethnic RSLs in chapter 6.

Meeting black and minority ethnic needs

Derby City Council is working closely with local RSLs to create a picture of housing need in the city. The council has developed a model to measure the scale of need in different parts of the city that draws on the council's own housing register and transfer list, as well as RSLs' registers. The model distinguishes between the needs of black (African and Caribbean), Asian (Indian, Pakistani and Bangladeshi) and white households.

The results of the research, which is still ongoing, show areas of the city where there is a need for more social housing targeted at black and minority ethnic communities, including dwellings with four or more bedrooms.

The council is seeking to meet black and minority ethnic needs that have been identified by:

- Supporting bids to the Housing Corporation for new schemes from RSLs, including black and minority ethnic RSLs
- Promoting existing housing, particularly sheltered housing in the inner city, to black and minority ethnic communities

The council runs housing advice sessions in community centres and in the council's home improvement centre. Advisers are able to communicate in other languages. A promotional leaflet about one of the council's schemes has recently been produced and it is available in Urdu, Hindi and Punjabi, as well as English. Photographs used in the leaflet reflect the ethnic mix of current tenants and of those living in the surrounding area. A local black and minority ethnic led RSL has also advised the council on the recruitment of a warden for a sheltered housing scheme located in a multi-racial area of the city.

The report of the Social Exclusion Unit's Policy Action Team on Unpopular Housing (DETR, 1999e) cites evidence of overcrowded black and minority ethnic households in poor quality housing alongside areas of empty, often better quality, housing stock. The report points out that there are barriers to access by minority communities of that stock – it may not be their preferred tenure and the communities may not feel safe there. There are, however, opportunities here. Regeneration of these low demand areas, perhaps involving tenure diversification, coupled with effective anti-harassment and support strategies, can create new areas where black and minority ethnic people will want to live.

■ Tenure

Housing organisations should be sensitive to tenure issues. In part, tenure reflects preferences – some prefer to rent, others prefer to buy. However, whilst some people may prefer owner occupation, they are not always able to afford full ownership.

RSLs providing homes for sale through low cost ownership schemes should consider the need to provide suitable housing, in terms of location, size and type, targeted at black and minority ethnic communities. Because some black and minority ethnic groups have lower incomes than the average, it may be necessary to offer the option of buying lower shares of the equity than would normally be offered – perhaps 25% sale/75% rent.

Requirements for owner occupied housing may also be met by private developers. Based on evidence of need, local authorities should discuss with private builders the mix of homes they provide. There may well be particular opportunities to address black and minority ethnic needs through negotiations with developers within the framework of 'affordable housing' policies.

Where the local authority is selling land for housing, it can have an even greater influence on the type of homes provided. For example, several authorities have included in development briefs accompanying land sales to developers the requirement that a proportion of homes be of the larger type that are suitable for some black and minority ethnic households.

■ Type, size and design

The extent to which housing is suitable for the people who will live in it is affected by a number of factors, including its type, size and design.

Many local studies of housing need have found acute shortages of larger accommodation (with four or more bedrooms) for black and minority ethnic communities, particularly Asian communities.

RSL new build programmes provide an opportunity to reduce such shortages. Such programmes require close liaison between local authorities and the Housing Corporation/Scottish Homes/National Assembly for Wales over the way that funding is targeted. In some local authority areas in England, agreement is reached about targeting a proportion of the Housing Corporation's Approved Development Programme each year for the provision of homes for larger households.

Consultation should also take place between local authorities and RSLs about the mix of homes to be provided on individual sites and, wherever possible, the opportunities to provide suitable homes for black and minority ethnic communities should be seized. Joint commissioning arrangements should make this process easier.

In addition to new build, there are other methods of delivering larger dwellings, as well as other housing, suitable for black and minority ethnic communities:

- Conversion of lofts or attics to bedrooms
- Targeting empty homes strategies at bringing houses back into use in areas in demand by black and minority ethnic people
- Knocking two dwellings into one

- Incentive schemes aimed at encouraging under-occupying households to release larger dwellings

Advice about culturally sensitive design is available in the National Housing Federation's and Home Housing Trust's updated report *Accommodating Diversity* (1998). Guidance is also available on sheltered housing for older Asian people (Ashram Agency, 1997).

Culturally sensitive design

As long ago as 1992, **Taff Housing**, a RSL based in Cardiff, realised that the specification it used for bathrooms in new build and rehabilitation schemes was not appropriate to the cultural needs of some of its black and minority ethnic tenants. In some cultures, people prefer to wash by standing or sitting in a bath and pouring water over themselves, rather than sitting in a bath full of water. This can cause water to run down the walls, and often behind the seal between the bath and wall, and on to the floor.

The specification was amended in a number of ways, including providing for a larger area of wall tiling, the use of a more rigid bath framing to prevent movement of the seal between the bath and the wall and the use of vinyl sheet flooring with no joints. Where new dwellings were to be targeted at particular minority communities, purpose designed washing facilities, including showers with tiled dished floors were to be considered.

Accommodating Diversity contains a wealth of guidance about design, both at the level of the individual dwelling and the wider area. Guidance includes:

- Adaptable housing that can accommodate extended families but which can be changed over time, as circumstances change. For example, a pair of semi detached houses can be internally connected to accommodate an extended family with the possibility of the dwellings reverting to two completely separate units if necessary

- A living room that is separate from the dining room or dining area. As well as allowing for the various members of the household to partake in different activities at the same time, it also allows for men and women to sit separately when guests are present

- Kitchen arrangements that suit customs regarding cooking and diet, including preferences for gas cookers and the need for adequate storage space and mechanical ventilation

The Bromford Housing Group has built an adaptable house for a large family in a development in Dudley. The house comprises a pair of semi detached houses which has been combined to form a single unit to accommodate a particular family. The unit can be changed back to a traditional pair of semi detached houses should the need arise in the future.

Providing housing: what should be monitored

✔ In the case of RSL dwellings, a comparison between the ethnic profile of tenants actually let dwellings in new schemes and the forecast profile made by the RSL when bidding for funding

✔ Ethnic profile of residents of schemes for rent and for sale that are targeted at specific black and minority ethnic communities

❏ Community regeneration

Black and minority ethnic communities are more likely, on average, to be living in deprived areas and so may well be affected by regeneration projects. However, while the communities have often been at the 'receiving end' of regeneration, they have not been adequately involved in planning or implementing urban renewal programmes. Furthermore, black and minority ethnic community organisations have often not been successful in securing funding for targeted projects. In the first three rounds of the Single Regeneration Budget, out of 555 successful bids, only four projects were led by black and minority ethnic organisations (Department of Land Economy, University of Cambridge, 1998; Chahal, 2000).

Areas with predominantly local authority housing, areas of mainly private housing, and mixed tenure neighbourhoods can all be affected by social exclusion. The link between deprivation and council housing is much weaker among the black and minority ethnic population. Deprived households from the white community are more heavily concentrated in council housing than deprived households from the black and minority ethnic population. Therefore, if a disproportionate amount of regeneration funding is allocated to areas of council housing, black and minority ethnic communities could be disadvantaged (Lee and Murie, 1997).

The government's focus on the need to tackle social exclusion has given renewed impetus to regeneration strategies both nationally and locally. The Social Exclusion Unit report *Bringing Britain Together* draws attention to important social divisions that exist across the country – divisions between areas that have benefited from rising living standards and the poorest neighbourhoods that have become run down, prone to crime and cut off from the labour market. The government's strategy for poor neighbourhoods will be based on:

- Investing in people, not buildings
- Involving communities, not parachuting in solutions
- Developing integrated approaches with clear leadership
- Ensuring mainstream policies really work for the poorest neighbourhoods
- Making long-term commitment with sustained political priority

(Social Exclusion Unit, 1998, p.10)

In April 2000, the Social Exclusion Unit's Policy Action Team 4 published a new set of proposals relating to neighbourhood management (Social Exclusion Unit, 2000b). The proposals are intended to achieve the goal of the national strategy for neighbourhood renewal based on the establishment of neighbourhood management projects. These projects adopt a number of principles:

- Someone with overall responsibility at the neighbourhood level
- Community involvement and leadership
- The tools to get things done – agreements with local service providers, devolved services and purchasing, ability to put pressure on agencies and government, and spending special resources
- A systematic, planned approach to tackling local problems
- Effective delivery mechanisms

The report proposes that special attention be given to the needs of black and minority ethnic communities in areas that are to be selected to test out approaches to neighbourhood management (pathfinder schemes). It recommends that all pathfinders should carry out ethnic monitoring and evaluation and, wherever possible, should draw on the experience and expertise of the black and minority ethnic voluntary sector. It further recommends that the pathfinder programme should include several areas with large black and minority ethnic populations and that, where the black and minority ethnic population is 80% or more, the pathfinder scheme should be led by people from these communities. In other areas, there should be proper levels of representation and involvement of black and minority ethnic communities.

■ Inclusive strategies for black and minority ethnic communities

Inclusive strategies for regeneration should be based on:

- Sound methods for choosing areas to receive regeneration programmes, based on sensitive analysis of need
- Full opportunities for black and minority ethnic people to be involved in designing regeneration strategies
- Involving black and minority ethnic run organisations, including black and minority ethnic RSLs, in the implementation of the strategy
- Giving consideration to ways in which employment opportunities can be created by regeneration projects, such as through local labour agreements and training schemes

Regeneration partnership

In 1999, two black and minority ethnic RSLs (Black Star and Hammac) and three mainstream RSLs (Focus, Family and Midland Area) established a trust with the aim of spearheading the regeneration of the multi-racial Handsworth area of Birmingham. Known as the **Handsworth Area Regeneration Trust**, the initiative is working with a range of organisations to improve prospects for employment, housing education and environment in the area. Action is centred on seven themes:

- Restoring pride
- Engaging neighbourhoods
- 'Having your say'
- Promoting stability
- Investing in employability
- 'Cleaner and safer'
- Raising standards

The trust commissioned a baseline audit which has identified the priority neighbourhoods and needs of the area and is embarking on a major local consultation exercise.

The trust is seeking to widen its membership by involving a range of businesses, statutory and voluntary partners, including Birmingham City Council, local colleges and the Aston Re-investment Trust.

Specific action points can be found in race equality guidance for the New Deal for Communities (NDC) programme. The guidance is comprehensive and recommends a number of measures to ensure that people from black and minority ethnic communities are involved in the work of NDC partnerships:

- Carrying out a mapping exercise on the potential for black and minority ethnic communities to become involved
- Involving black and minority ethnic communities at all levels of decision-making and delivery
- Consulting on an ongoing basis to obtain the views of black and minority ethnic communities
- Monitoring the inclusiveness of the partnership
- Adopting capacity building measures to help people develop the skills and experience they need to get involved
- Using networks associated with black and minority ethnic groups to encourage wider participation
- Including team building and equal opportunities training for NDC board members, using outside help where necessary
- Considering allocating specific funding or taking positive action to ensure black and minority ethnic participation

The report also stresses organisations should avoid only asking black and minority ethnic groups to address 'race' issues and should avoid tokenism – partners and communities need resources and support if they are to have a real influence.

(DETR, 2000b)

Partnerships catering for diversity

St. Martins estate in the **London Borough of Lambeth** has a black and minority ethnic population of over 45% and young people under 25 account for just under half of the residents. One key objective in the regeneration process has been to secure the involvement of all households living on the estate to ensure that all communities share the benefits of participation and of improved living.

Presentation Housing Association, a black and minority ethnic RSL, has been involved in the consultation of residents. The active and competent involvement of a black and minority ethnic RSL in the regeneration of the estate has several important benefits:

- It has helped to tackle exclusion of black and minority ethnic communities and has had long term benefits in creating integrated and cohesive communities
- It has provided sustainable models for community development and regeneration work
- Effective and successful partnerships have been formed which provide examples for others
- It promotes wider socio-economic empowerment in black and minority ethnic communities and helps to raise the self esteem of individuals

(*Housing Today*, 7 January 1999)

Community regeneration: what should be monitored

✔ Ethnic profile of populations in areas that are receiving regeneration programmes

✔ Ethnic profile of residents participating in consultation exercises, compared with profile of residents in the area affected by the regeneration programme

✔ Comparison between the success rates of funding bids from black and minority ethnic organisations and from mainstream organisations

✔ Ethnic profile of people taking up new jobs and training opportunities created in the area, compared with ethnic profile of people locally who are unemployed

❏ Improving conditions in private sector housing

The English House Condition Survey has demonstrated that black and minority ethnic people are over-represented in poor quality private housing (DETR, 1998). Local authorities, together with their partners, need to develop effective policies to tackle problems of disrepair and poor amenities, particularly in inner urban areas where many minority communities are concentrated. Programmes to provide grant aid and other practical support to owners of poor quality housing should form an essential part of the local housing strategy and, provided they are carried out in a culturally sensitive way, they should contribute to meeting black and minority ethnic needs.

Because of concentrations of many black and minority ethnic communities in poor quality private housing, decisions that local authorities make about the level of capital expenditure to be targeted at private housing, as opposed to council housing and other programmes, have an important 'race' dimension. This is a particularly critical issue in view of the introduction of a single housing capital 'pot'. Authorities should have a rationale for deciding on spending priorities that bears scrutiny and which is heavily influenced by relative need. Authorities should consider the need for cross tenure stock condition surveys as these could help form the basis for rational decisions on spending priorities.

Local authorities, in partnership with other organisations where appropriate, need to consider the following action:

- Development of effective strategies to renovate areas of poor quality private housing through such programmes as renovation grants, group repair schemes, equity release schemes, especially for older people, and environmental improvements

- Setting up schemes to help owners repair and maintain their homes, for example handypersons schemes, maintenance services, home maintenance surveys and publishing lists of builders that meet certain defined criteria. There may be scope for black and minority ethnic led organisations to provide these services

- Involvement of RSLs, including where appropriate black and minority ethnic RSLs, in refurbishing housing for rent or for sale

The Housing Green Paper discusses a number of proposals regarding the improvement of older private sector housing, including new local authority powers to provide loans for home improvement, more flexibility over grant aid and quality mark schemes for builders (DETR, 2000c).

All programmes need to be sensitive to the requirements of black and minority ethnic communities, including provision for those whose first language is not English. Authorities and their partners should provide opportunities for the communities to be involved in designing the solutions.

Questions of housing design are important. For example, the requirement for two living rooms should be respected (see section above on providing housing) and converting second living rooms to kitchens or bedrooms should be avoided as far as possible.

In some areas, older housing cannot be refurbished at an economic cost and clearance is the only answer. Clearance creates anxiety and uncertainties for all residents, but some people within the black and minority ethnic communities may feel uncertainties particularly acutely because of worries that they will be rehoused in an area away from their own community. Owners may also be particularly anxious to remain owner occupiers.

Local authorities engaging in clearance should be particularly mindful of these kinds of anxieties. Regular consultation and information giving are essential. Opportunities for local rehousing should be provided and, where appropriate, this should include ownership options through, for example shared ownership schemes or the use of relocation grants. Clearance may have to be phased in order to maximise the possibility of local rehousing for people who want it.

Improving conditions in private sector housing: what should be monitored

✔ A comparison between the ethnic profile of applicants for renovation grants with a profile of the community living in substandard housing

✔ A comparison between the number of renovation grants offered to each ethnic group and the number of applications for grants from each ethnic group

❑ Services for homeless people

Homelessness is a key factor in social exclusion and it disproportionately affects black and minority ethnic groups. In London, nearly 50% of all people who become statutorily homeless are from black and minority ethnic groups (Carter, 1998). Black and minority ethnic people are more likely to be living in temporary accommodation with friends and relatives (O'Mahony and Ferguson, 1991; Daly, 1996) than sleeping on the streets or staying in night shelters (Carter, 1998).

Carter (1998) found that homeless black and minority ethnic people were less likely to use a day centre or to come into contact with an outreach team. They were, however, more likely to use this type of service if it was for young people, women or targeted at black and minority ethnic groups. Racist harassment can act as a barrier to black and minority ethnic people using hostels, and housing organisations must take this issue on board when developing a service for homeless people.

Young homeless people from black and minority ethnic communities have a strong preference for hostel accommodation provided by black and minority ethnic organisations as a step to their own rented accommodation. (O'Mahony and Ferguson, 1991).

■ Developing a responsive service

Housing services have a wide role to play in challenging homelessness and encouraging black and minority ethnic homeless people to access mainstream and specialist services. An effective response should be based on a proper assessment of need, using research methods that are sensitive to the issue of 'hidden homelessness' manifested by the unwillingness of many people to use existing homelessness agencies. Consultation with homeless people and with current service providers is also essential.

As with provision for other groups with specific needs, there are two questions to be asked about the policy response:

- In what ways can current provision be made more sensitive to black and minority ethnic people?
- Is there a need for specific provision targeted at particular black and minority ethnic communities?

These questions are discussed more fully in the section on services for people with care and support needs.

Small and Hinton (1997) argue that developing an effective and fair service that meets both the housing and health care needs of black and minority ethnic single homeless people requires the following approaches:

- An assessment of the numbers and characteristics of minority ethnic homeless people within a given local area
- An analysis of the views of homeless people themselves, and of the agencies working with them
- Increasing expertise about minority ethnic issues and promoting the appropriateness, accessibility and adaptability of the service
- Developing long term working relationships with community groups
- Working with hostels
- Working with mainstream primary health care services to improve their appropriateness, accessibility and acceptability
- Developing a strategy to provide information about registration and access to a full range of services
- Developing an ongoing consultation process
- Monitoring and evaluation

Services to homeless people: what should be monitored

✔ A comparison of the ethnic origins of people applying as homeless, accepted as homeless and accommodated in various types of housing – hostels, bed and breakfast, permanent accommodation

✔ A comparison between the various ethnic groups of the length of time homeless people spend in temporary accommodation

❑ Housing advice and information

Many local authorities, and some other organisations, provide housing advice and information services.

It is important that the ethnic origin of users of these services is monitored in order to see whether:

- Black and minority ethnic people are using the service to the degree expected, given the numbers within the local population or other indicators of need

- There are patterns in the problems that are presented. Trends in the figures may suggest the need for new housing provision, or some other policy response.

Low levels of take-up of the service by black and minority ethnic people may indicate the need for publicity campaigns. Housing organisations should also consider the need for advisory services targeted at particular communities. Voluntary organisations serving particular minority communities could be funded to provide such services.

Housing consumers are not the only groups that need advice and information. Landlords may not appreciate the complexity of the law on such matters as disrepair and security of tenure. Local authorities should consider the need for targeted publicity campaigns and for training for landlords. Some authorities run consultative forums for landlords. Particular efforts should be made to ensure that black and minority ethnic landlords are represented in such forums.

Housing information and advice: what should be monitored

✔ Breakdown of the ethnic origin of people seeking advice and information, compared with a breakdown of the ethnic origin of households in the local area or households known to have housing needs

❏ Services for people with care and support needs

Strategies to provide care and support should be based on a full understanding of needs and on developing appropriate, culturally sensitive services. Many people with care and support needs live in ordinary housing, whilst others live in specialist housing, such as sheltered schemes. Local housing and community care strategies normally aim to provide a range of services – from support to people in their current homes, through to various kinds of specialist housing with varying levels of care and support. Given this range of provision, and consumer choice – at least to some degree – service providers need to make sure that people from black and minority ethnic communities enjoy the same amount of choice as those in the majority population.

Useful general advice about housing and support is available in the CIH Good Practice Briefing No. 16 *Housing and Services for People with Support Needs* (1999).

■ The importance of research and consultation

It is important that those providing services for black and minority ethnic communities engage in effective consultation with the communities in order to ensure, not only that the services themselves are designed in a way that is sensitive to needs, but also to make sure that the services are properly marketed.

Alongside effective consultation processes is the need for research and monitoring on what is happening locally. Appropriate provision for black and minority communities should be underpinned by three kinds of research:

- Research into unmet needs among black and minority ethnic communities and, wherever possible, projections of future need
- Monitoring the level of take-up of existing services by the various communities
- Monitoring consumer satisfaction about current provision. Monitoring mechanisms should allow for comparisons to be made between the views of people of different ethnic origins to help identify whether there is a need for service improvements targeted at particular groups

■ Joint planning

Good arrangements for joint planning between all of the agencies involved in care and support services are essential. Access by black and minority ethnic communities to appropriate services should be one of the core themes running through the joint planning process.

The CRE report on *Race, Culture and Community Care,* which was written with the assistance of the Chartered Institute of Housing and the National Health Service Confederation, says that health and local authorities have experimented with a number of ways to ensure that black and minority ethnic interests are represented in community care provision:

- Minority ethnic planning advisers
- Minority ethnic user and carer representatives on joint planning groups
- Partnership committees or separate consultative groups of minority ethnic users and carers and minority ethnic provider organisations
- Specific joint planning groups for minority ethnic issues
- Users, carers and staff from minority ethnic groups monitoring the work of joint planning groups
- Sponsoring independent minority ethnic advocacy organisations
- Surveys of minority ethnic users' and carers' views
- 'Search' conferences enabling minority ethnic participants to contribute to service review and development

(CRE, 1997, p. 35)

New proposals under the Government's *Supporting People* policy will bring about significant changes in the way in which support to vulnerable people is funded from 2003. In England, the element of housing benefit which covers support will be merged with RSLs' Supported Housing Management Grant in a new specific budget. This budget will be allocated to local authorities on the basis of need, and housing, social services and probation will administer the fund locally. The new arrangements will be applied differently in Scotland and Wales. However, throughout the country the new responsibilities placed on local agencies will require even closer collaboration than in the past. The arrangements presuppose a thorough understanding of support needs in the community and agreement about the kind of support services that are required. It is essential that the reviews carried out in preparation for the *Supporting People* arrangements are sensitive to differences in need and, in particular, to the requirements of people from black and minority ethnic communities. DETR consultation papers remind authorities to consider the needs of black and minority ethnic communities, for example when evaluating existing service provision in their area and when planning consultation of service users.

Housing providers can get involved in planning appropriate care and support services in several ways. These include:

- Housing representatives participating in care and support planning groups
- Establishing an inter-agency forum with a specific 'housing, care and support' remit
- Arrangements in which housing representatives make a contribution to the community care plan and social services/social work and health representatives make contributions to the housing strategy/housing plan/housing strategies and operational plans

■ Specialist housing and support services

Some providers of housing with support point out that take-up is low among members of the black and minority ethnic communities. Adrian Jones' research (1994) on sheltered housing and black and minority ethnic elders asked RSLs to identify possible barriers to access by older people from black and minority ethnic communities to sheltered housing. A number of barriers were suggested:

- Image of the providers and the schemes themselves – schemes were thought to be for white people and the RSLs were identified as 'white providers'
- The schemes were in the wrong area
- Black and minority ethnic people feared that they would be isolated if they moved to the scheme
- The design was felt to be inappropriate
- There were problems of affordability
- There were language problems

As the black and minority ethnic population ages, it will be important to plan in particular for increased provision of appropriate housing and support for older people.

Changing what is already there

If local research identifies unmet need for housing and support services for one or more of the black and minority ethnic communities, then attention needs to be focused on the best way to respond to that need. The response should not be confined to new provision options alone. Existing provision may have an important role to play.

In relation to sheltered housing, Jones (1994) argues for a thorough review of current practice within the existing sheltered stock to make sure that schemes are able to cater for black and minority ethnic elders. Similar approaches should be adopted for specialist provision targeted at other client groups. A range of action is recommended. These relate both to the schemes themselves and to the organisation which manages them:

- Employment of more black and minority ethnic staff

- Staff training in equal opportunities

- Working with existing tenants to inform them of the organisation's approach to equal opportunities and to promote the benefits of ethnically mixed schemes

- Working to make sure that the ethnic profile of management committees reflects the communities which the organisation is seeking to serve

- Working with black and minority ethnic RSLs – possibly transferring mainstream stock to these organisations

- Increasing awareness in the minority communities of the services that are available

- Setting targets for lettings to people from black and minority ethnic communities

(Jones, 1994)

New provision

Local research may reveal the need for new provision of housing and support services for some of the black and minority ethnic communities. It is important that the response to such needs is not constrained by existing models of provision. For example:

- It cannot be assumed that African Caribbean elders want sheltered housing based on the British model with the only difference that it has a black warden

- Where supported housing is provided for Asian people, relatives of those living there may feel it their duty to take on a share of the care and support that is needed. Providing organisations will need to make arrangements for this

- Some Irish people prefer shared, rather than self contained, housing because it offers companionship and support (Randall and Brown, 1997)

Many people from the black and minority ethnic communities, just as from the white community, will prefer to live in their own home, with support, rather than move to specialist accommodation. In many areas, for example, social services authorities are contracting with black and minority ethnic care organisations to provide culturally sensitive home-based support and care services.

In some areas, research will reveal the need for new supported or sheltered housing schemes targeted at particular minority ethnic groups. There are strong arguments that such provision should be made, or managed, by a black and minority ethnic led organisation. However, this will not always be feasible as, for instance, a black and minority ethnic RSL may not exist locally.

Regardless of the identity of the provider, there are a number of essential prerequisites to culturally sensitive housing and support:

- Proper research into need

- Effective consultation with the community

- Full support from all the relevant agencies, including housing, social services/social work and health. Agreements about funding nominations, referrals and assessments will need to be negotiated

- Finding a location where the targeted group will wish to live

- Design that is sensitive to needs

- Management, care and support services that are sensitive to needs

- Effective local networking and publicity to ensure the scheme is known to people who may need it

Meeting specific needs

In 1997, the **City and County of Cardiff** commissioned research into the housing needs of black and minority ethnic elders. The research concentrated on needs and on current housing provision. Amongst other findings, the research discovered that take-up of sheltered housing was low among black and minority ethnic elders due to:

- Lack of awareness of what is available
- A belief that sheltered housing involves a loss of independence
- Belief that sheltered schemes are for white people

The research also highlighted acute housing need within the Somali community – particularly among single older people who tend to have no family to support them. Many lived in lodging houses.

The council is now working with a RSL to draw up plans to provide a small housing scheme comprising 15 flats which will be targeted at older Somali men. It will be built in an area where many Somalis live and which is near a mosque and halal butchers. Consultation with the local community revealed the importance of a meeting room – referred to as a 'café' – and this will be provided as part of the scheme.

The council is also working in partnership with a RSL to provide a scheme targeted at the Yemeni community. The scheme is likely to comprise a mixture of flats for older people and houses for families.

Gloucester City Council commissioned research into the needs of African Caribbean elders which demonstrated the need for specific provision for the community and also highlighted the need to encourage people from the community to apply for services that are provided. **Hanover Housing Association** has since built a sheltered housing scheme targeted at African Caribbean people and as a result of a publicity campaign mounted to bring the scheme to the attention of the community, one-third of the flats have been occupied by African-Caribbean tenants.

During the development and promotion of the scheme, a steering group of representatives from the community met regularly with the council and Hanover. Nehemiah Housing Association acted as advisers to the community throughout. The steering group is now working towards providing services within the scheme, such as a luncheon club which could benefit both tenants and the wider community. Other services that could be provided are catering and landscaping work.

Local authorities should consider carefully whether traditional nomination arrangements are appropriate for specialist provision targeted at particular minority ethnic communities. Given that such provision may be aimed at 'filling gaps' that existing providers have failed to meet, it is possible that local authority waiting lists, or other traditional sources, will not identify people with the needs that such schemes are seeking to meet. Authorities may therefore wish to consider waiving normal nominations requirements, or negotiate lower targets with the accommodation providers.

Survey results

Specific provision for black and minority ethnic communities

✎ A quarter of local authorities provide particular housing schemes and services that are targeted to meet the needs of black and minority ethnic communities. This provision includes sheltered housing, specialist advisory and support services and anti-harassment services.

Services for people with care and support needs: what should be monitored

✔ Profile of ethnic origin of service users, as far as possible compared with the profile of people within the age/population groups in the community as a whole for whom the services are intended

❏ Services for refugees and asylum seekers

The Immigration and Asylum Act 1999 brought about major changes in policy for asylum seekers. The implications stretch far beyond housing because there are changes to welfare benefits and to responsibilities for providing for this group. The Home Office has now become responsible for co-ordinating the provision of accommodation. The responsibilities will be discharged via the National Asylum Support Service which will contract with a range of accommodation providers locally: local authorities, RSLs, voluntary organisations and private landlords. The Act has removed local authorities' responsibilities under the homelessness legislation to asylum seekers who claim asylum after 2 April 2000, but local authorities will be expected to help in the provision of accommodation wherever possible under the new contracting arrangements.

Detailed guidance on housing and support services for asylum seekers is contained in a report by the Housing Corporation (Zetter and Pearl, 1999a). Although the guidance is targeted at RSLs, much of it could apply equally to local authorities and other providers. The guidance sets out a checklist of indicators to help decide whether housing is suitable for asylum seekers. 'Plus factors' regarding the area in which accommodation should be situated include: multi-racial areas, areas with cultural and religious facilities, an active voluntary sector in the area, ready access to primary health care, the property being within a manageable distance from an area office and the presence of a local office with resources and experience to deal with asylum seekers.

The guide sets out good practice in relation to support packages. Basic principles include 'joined up', rather than piecemeal, provision and inter-agency co-operation. Support needs should be systematically assessed and provided on a comprehensive basis. The responsibilities of the various agencies should be clearly laid down in protocols.

Key questions

- *Are services based on a proper understanding of need and on full consultation with service users and potential service users?*

- *Have all available opportunities to meet the needs of black and minority ethnic communities been thoroughly explored?*

- *Is the organisation's approach to regeneration based on the principles of inclusiveness set out in this chapter?*

- *Are the requirements set out in the* **Supporting People** *arrangements being taken as an opportunity to review the appropriateness of care and support services for black and minority ethnic people?*

Chapter 5

Aiming for Race Equality: Services for Tenants and Potential Tenants

This chapter discusses:
- Allocation of housing
- Dealing with anti-social behaviour
- Tackling racist harassment
- Repairs and improvements

❑ Allocation of housing

Discrimination and disadvantage affect black and minority ethnic people in relation to the allocation of housing in a number of ways. These can reflect the inappropriateness of current provision and services and a failure on the part of landlords to communicate effectively with the communities concerned. Disadvantage can stem from the fact that:

- Black and minority ethnic people may not know what is available and may feel that the organisation does not have the sort of housing they want, or does not have housing in the areas they want.

- Black and minority ethnic people may believe that they will not be treated fairly or sensitively by the organisation if they apply for housing.

- The organisation may not have communicated properly about the process of applying for, and obtaining, a home. For example, black and minority ethnic applicants may not realise the importance the organisation attaches to medical circumstances in the allocation of housing and may fail to include sufficient detail about ill health within the family on the application form. Having applied, black and minority ethnic people may not realise the need to keep in touch with the landlord if they move or if other circumstances change.

• Rules governing access to housing may indirectly discriminate if they have a disproportionate and unjustifiable effect on black and minority ethnic people. For example, stipulations on the length of time an applicant must have lived within an area or rules denying access to owner occupiers may have such an effect.

• Systems that apply priorities to different groups of applicants may discriminate against black and minority ethnic people. For example, if African Caribbean people are over-represented among those who are found to be homeless, they will face disadvantage overall if homeless applicants are offered poorer quality properties, compared with other groups of applicants. Allocation schemes that do not give sufficient weight to overcrowded households may disadvantage Asian households who tend, on average, to be more overcrowded than other groups of households.

The Housing Green Paper sets out a number of proposals for changing the way that social housing is let. The broad aims of the proposals are to empower people to make decisions over where they live, to help create sustainable communities and to encourage effective use of the social housing stock (DETR, 2000c).

■ Aiming for race equality in housing allocations

Attention needs to be focused on fair policies and procedures throughout the process. It is not simply a question of each organisation getting its own processes right. Local authorities and RSLs will need to work together to devise non-discriminatory systems in relation to nominations. Authorities will need to ensure that all housing applicants are aware of the existence of the nominations route to RSL housing so that they can opt to be considered for this if they wish. It should be borne in mind that some people who apply to the local authority for housing will not know what RSLs are and may be confused when they receive offers from RSLs. Local authorities and RSLs should ensure a full two-way flow of information about applicants' needs and preferences. Nominations made and outcomes, in terms of offers, lettings and refusals, should be an integral part of ethnic monitoring.

Survey results

Access to housing

- Eligibility of owner occupiers to go on the housing register: 42% of authorities have no restrictions, 27% allow them to register if they are in need, 22% allow them to register if in need and they have equity below a certain level. Only 2% of authorities have a blanket ban on owners registering. The remaining 7% allow owners to register subject to a variety of restrictions.

- Residence/work qualifications on access to the housing register: 30% of authorities have no residence/work restrictions, 44% say applicants can register if they live or work in the area, 26% say they can register if they live/work in the area for a certain period of time (mostly six months or a year).

- 31% of authorities said that, compared with other applicants on the housing register, homeless households tend to get less choice of housing or poorer quality housing.

- 11% of authorities said that, compared with transfer cases, non homeless applicants on the housing register tend to get less choice of housing or poorer quality housing.

- 24% of authorities operate a local lettings or community lettings policy for part of their housing stock.

- Authorities with community lettings schemes were asked what safeguards they had put in place to prevent unfair discrimination against black and minority ethnic communities as a result of the schemes. Some authorities pointed out that the schemes were still based on need. Few others gave much detail about safeguards. Some simply mentioned ethnic monitoring of lettings.

Note: stock transfer authorities are excluded from the above figures

- 17% of authorities said they have taken some special initiative to improve black and minority ethnic people's access to their own or RSLs' housing

- Examples of initiatives taken to improve access include counselling about the availability of housing in different areas, establishment of tenant support schemes to reduce isolation and, in areas where there are few black and minority ethnic tenants, making offers to several minority ethnic applicants at the same time with the aim that, if the offers are accepted, households can provide mutual support.

Raising awareness

Housing organisations should make sure that people in housing need are aware of the housing and other services that they offer. Where the ethnic profile of those taking up tenancies does not match the profile of people who are in need in the community, as measured by the Census or social surveys, then the reasons for this should be investigated.

Promoting services among black and minority ethnic communities

Three Scottish RSLs, **Kirk Care, Hanover (Scotland)** and **Bield Housing Association**, which specialise in the provision of housing with support and care, commissioned Positive Action in Housing to carry out research into the level and nature of need for sheltered housing amongst older people from black and minority ethnic communities (Positive Action in Housing, 1999).

The research was carried out in Glasgow and Edinburgh and involved interviewing older people and focus groups with people from black and minority ethnic communities. It also analysed current levels of housing provision for black and minority ethnic older people. The report arising from the research recommended the appointment of a development worker to work with these communities to raise their awareness of the services provided by the RSLs.

As a result of the research, the three RSLs have jointly appointed a housing equal opportunities officer. The officer's role is to:
- Network with the black and minority ethnic communities to encourage take-up of services
- To improve employment of people from the communities
- To set up facilities for instant access to community language resources
- To facilitate translation of documents into community languages
- To develop a 'Happy to Translate' logo that organisations would include on their letterheads, leaflets and other literature

There are a number of ways of raising awareness of what organisations have to offer. They include leaflets, audio tapes and videos, and methods that involve outreach to the communities such as seminars, exhibitions and networking with community organisations. This topic is discussed further in the section on communication in chapter 3.

Access to social housing by black and minority ethnic communities

Glasgow City Council has adopted an action plan which seeks to improve black and minority ethnic communities' access to its housing. The plan involves:

- Increasing the number of front line staff who can speak other languages by designating 10 housing officer and assistant housing officer posts for suitably qualified applicants who can speak Punjabi, Urdu, Hindi or Chinese.

- Increasing information to black and minority ethnic communities about housing opportunities through profiles of the available housing stock in different areas of the city and through open days, a 'road show' to secondary schools and by networking with community organisations.

- The introduction of anti-racist training for staff. Two training and development workers have been appointed to provide this training.

- A survey of black and minority ethnic tenants and applicants to obtain information about experiences and preferences. The survey aims to find out how the council could improve access to its housing by black and minority ethnic communities.

Dealing with enquiries and applications

An efficient two-way flow of information at the initial enquiry stage is essential to a fair housing allocation process. This can be enhanced through:

- The provision of clear and comprehensive information, using accessible formats in plain, everyday language. Leaflets should be written with people's information needs in mind.

- A clear application form that prompts people to provide all of the relevant information.

- Access to staff who can speak the appropriate languages or speedy access to interpreting services.

- Advice about options. Black and minority ethnic people, who are perhaps less familiar with a district than other people, or who want to live in areas they know, may name fewer areas than white applicants. Applicants who name only a few areas where they would consider housing should be informed about other areas where they may stand more chance of a speedy offer. However, care should be taken to ensure black and minority ethnic people are not simply steered towards low demand areas. Options about being nominated to a RSL or about buying a shared ownership home should also be explored.

- Explanation about the process. For example: if applicants to a local authority are likely to be nominated to a RSL, are they aware that this might happen? Do they know what a RSL is?

- Providing details of a named person who can be contacted if there are queries.

Assessing need

Eligibility requirements and systems that rank priorities for allocations should not directly discriminate on the basis of race; neither should they discriminate indirectly.

Denying access to housing to people who have not lived in a district for a certain length of time or to people who currently own their homes could be indirectly discriminatory under the Race Relations Act 1976. In Scotland, local authorities are prohibited by the Housing (Scotland) Act 1987 from denying access to owner occupiers to their lists.

Systems for assessing priorities amongst those accepted for housing should seek to reflect the needs that exist in the community and should be checked to ensure they do not indirectly discriminate. Proposed changes to allocation schemes, for example changing the weight given to different aspects of need, should be carefully modelled to ensure that there are no unintentional and discriminatory consequences.

There are several dimensions to the disadvantage that may be suffered by some or all of the black and minority ethnic communities if systems have not been devised fairly.

- They may receive a lower number of offers or lettings than could reasonably be expected on the basis of their numbers on the housing register, or the numbers of people in the wider community who are in need

- They may have to wait longer on average for offers or lettings, compared with other groups

- They may receive poorer quality offers or lettings, compared with other groups

- They may only receive offers in certain areas

- They may not be aware of certain services that may be available, such as decoration allowances or tenancy support services

Particular care should be given to:

- The priority given, and the quality of homes offered, to new applicants for housing and to current tenants who wish to transfer. If there is a lower proportion of black and minority ethnic people amongst current tenants than amongst new applicants, allocation schemes that give undue preference to transfers could be indirectly discriminatory.

- Whether there is any discrimination in the priority given to split households. For example, is an applicant with a daughter living in India, and who will join the family on rehousing, treated the same as an applicant with a daughter living elsewhere in the United Kingdom?

- Whether the priorities given to people who suffer ill health recognise diseases that only affect, or disproportionately affect, black and minority ethnic people, such as sickle cell anaemia.

- Decisions about 'special cases'. Are the grounds for the use of discretion clearly set out? Are members of staff who make discretionary allocations suitably trained? Is there an appeal mechanism?

- Taking account of patterns of racist harassment. In areas where there have been particular problems, incoming tenants should be offered support.

Making offers

Just as at the initial enquiry stage, efficient two-way communication is essential at the offer stage.

Applicants need to understand what they are being offered. Particular care will be needed to explain to someone whose first language is not English, the nature of the dwelling, what facilities exist locally, the support that may be available (for example regular housing officer visits for an initial period), any financial help that may be available (for example for decoration) and what the consequences are if the offer is refused.

People who are unfamiliar with an area may need longer to decide whether to accept an offer of accommodation. They may, for example, need to investigate routes to work and schools. Black and minority ethnic people may make up a larger proportion of such applicants.

If the offer is refused, organisations need to find out why – there may be something that can be done to make the offer acceptable, but if not, clear reasons for refusal need to be recorded so that the next offer can be more suited to the applicant's needs and preferences. The ethnic origin of those refusing offers should be monitored, together with reasons for refusals, as this may yield valuable information about preferences. In particular, refusals on the grounds of fear of racist harassment should be regularly monitored as the information may help to target anti-harassment campaigns.

Many people from black and minority ethnic communities refuse offers in areas with which they are not familiar. The reasons for this are fully understandable: they may fear isolation and harassment. But it is of vital importance that housing organisations, in partnership with other organisations, open up housing opportunities for black and minority ethnic people, particularly in areas where housing may be more plentiful.

There are a number of ways in which opportunities can be improved:

- Effective action to tackle racist harassment. If there is a problem of harassment in a particular area, potential black and minority ethnic tenants should be informed of this and of the action the landlord has taken, and is continuing to take, to tackle it.

- Offering properties in the same area and at the same time to several black and minority ethnic households, and making sure that each household is aware that the others are being made the offers. Households are more likely to accept if there are likely to be people of the same background living nearby. This is usually more feasible in new developments where a number of properties can be offered at the same time.

- Efforts to support black and minority ethnic people in their new homes and make them feel comfortable in their new areas. Inclusive tenant participation strategies and community networks have a vital role to play here.

Eastern Shires Housing Association found that relatively few people from black and minority ethnic communities, particularly Asian communities, were applying for accommodation in its two single person blocks in Leicester. To help overcome this, it appointed a Community Development Manager to work with local communities to raise awareness about the services offered by the association. In addition, security in the blocks has been improved through the installation of a concierge service and closed circuit television cameras in the communal areas.

These changes appear to have resulted in an increase in the number of lettings made to black and minority ethnic people. The proportion of lettings by the association to black and minority ethnic people in Leicester has risen from 17% in 1994/95 to 37% in 1999/2000.

Moving into new areas

A project seeking to integrate black and minority ethnic people in new RSL developments, which were built in existing housing areas away from traditional areas of settlement by black and minority ethnic communities, has recently been evaluated by Joseph Rowntree Foundation funded research (Hawtin, Kettle, Moran and Crossley, 1999). This **Leeds** based project sought to encourage members of black and minority ethnic communities to widen the choice of areas in which they would live and to encourage tenant participation in the new community. It involved the appointment of a tenant participation co-ordinator, meetings with tenants prior to moving in order to discuss and to try to resolve any concerns they may have, support to tenants after moving in and encouragement to all tenants to join participation initiatives.

Among the lessons learned by the project were:

- Working closely with all newly selected tenants is essential
- The needs and aspirations of existing communities, where the new housing is to be built, should be integrated with the implementation of the project
- The image of incoming RSLs and the development needs careful promotion among existing residents
- Nominations systems need to be agreed early on and should be flexible
- All of the relevant agencies should be fully committed

Making the letting

Housing organisations should take particular care to make sure that people unfamiliar with social housing, or whose first language is not English, understand the nature of the agreement they are entering into and what their rights and responsibilities are. The attention of all of those who are signing up for a tenancy should be drawn to the anti-harassment clauses of the tenancy agreement – both to the sanctions that may be used against perpetrators and to the help given to victims. The report of Policy Action Team 8 on Anti-Social Behaviour contains a specific recommendation for social landlords that all tenancy agreements should contain non-harassment clauses, and should make clear the action that will be taken if these are breached.

■ Community or local lettings schemes

Some housing organisations are moving away from purely needs based allocations, at least for part of their housing stock. There are three main reasons why this is happening:

- In some areas, there are growing surpluses of social housing and it is, therefore, no longer a case of rationing scarce resources. The emphasis now is on finding tenants prepared to take tenancies rather than deciding who is in the most need of them.

- Some organisations are concerned that a purely needs-based approach leads to unbalanced communities with disproportionate numbers of, for example, benefit-dependant households. If account is taken of factors like existing family ties in an area, then, it is argued, communities may become more balanced and stable, and family members can provide more support to each other.

- Some organisations have started to deny access to people with criminal convictions or with a history of anti-social behaviour.

The move away from a needs-based approach towards policies with a greater focus on maintaining sustainable communities poses potential problems for race equality in housing allocations. Organisations contemplating the introduction of non-needs factors should proceed very carefully.

In low demand areas, efforts to find potential tenants should be as broadly based as possible. This would seem to be in the interests of both letting an empty dwelling quickly and complying with equal opportunity policies. Such approaches as advertising empty dwellings in the local paper, or displaying details in estate agents and shops and mailing details to advice centres and community organisations should reach a good cross-section of the potential demand.

A key concern is that community or local lettings schemes, which give weight to local connections, may exclude black and minority ethnic people from areas where they are already under-represented. It is vital that, before such schemes are introduced, the potential effects are carefully modelled to check whether discrimination would result. If it is decided to introduce such schemes, then a system of regular monitoring should be established. The Housing Green Paper emphasises the need to ensure that such policies are not unfairly discriminatory.

Care also needs to be taken about excluding certain people on the grounds of past misbehaviour. Firstly, such bans should only be contemplated in the case of *proven* misbehaviour. Secondly, there is the question of *relevance*. As the National Housing Federation's good practice guide on access and race equality (1998) points out, if past criminal convictions are allowed to bar people from getting housed, this could impact disproportionately and unfairly in some areas on young black men. Not all convictions are an indication that someone is likely to cause a nuisance. The Housing Green Paper states that the government intends to remove powers to impose blanket exclusions from housing registers. Temporary reductions in priority for those guilty of anti-social behaviour may, however, continue to be justified.

■ New approaches to letting social housing

There is growing interest in introducing more choice in the social housing allocation process. This stems from a number of factors, including a desire to empower housing consumers and to improve the image of social housing. The Housing Green Paper argues for a major shift in thinking in the way social housing is let. The paper argues that people need more than a property that is physically adequate to meet their needs. They need to live where they feel secure, perhaps close to family, friends, places of work and other amenities. The paper argues for greater weighting to be given to people's preferences for these kinds of factors.

The government is promoting a number of pilot projects of choice-based schemes by social landlords in the UK. The Delft Model is one example of the methods for introducing greater choice. It originated in the Dutch town of that name and is now used, with variations, by 80% of municipal authorities in Holland. Under the Delft Model, there are no housing allocations in the traditional sense in which landlords select households from their lists and offer dwellings to them. Instead, households who wish to move take the lead by responding to advertisements for vacant social rented dwellings in free newspapers delivered to all households in the area.

If more than one household requests a particular dwelling, priority is determined on the following basis:

- New applicants: in some areas in Holland priority is determined by the age of the household head – older people get priority. In other areas where there is a housing register, priority is given to those who have been on the list the longest
- Existing tenants: priority is determined by the length of the tenancy

Housing need is not a relevant factor in the majority of lettings. However, the model does cater for urgent cases, such as asylum seekers, refugees and homeless people. In some areas, a proportion of lettings is 'top sliced' for these groups. In other areas, households with an urgent need have a 'priority card' and their requests get precedence over normal cases.

The Delft model and others do present some timely challenges to housing providers. Compared with traditional arrangements, they allow for a greater degree of choice for those seeking housing. They give people wishing to move an active, rather than a merely passive, role and there is accountability: once a letting has been made, landlords publish details of the number of responses made and of the successful applicant.

However, the race equality implications of this approach need to be thought through carefully. The removal of need as a factor in the majority of lettings may well disadvantage groups who experience disproportionate need, as many black and minority ethnic communities do. In the United Kingdom, the use of age of head of household to determine priority is likely to be indirectly discriminatory because black and minority ethnic communities tend to have younger age profiles than the white community. Length of tenancy and length of time on the housing register will disadvantage newcomers to an area – which could again be indirectly discriminatory.

Any system which relies on rapid response to advertisements will need to have safeguards to ensure that those who cannot read English, or have difficulty in reading English, are not disadvantaged.

Clearly, the essential principles underlying these and other schemes – choice, an active role for consumers and accountability – could be combined with a needs-based system. Although the Housing Green Paper warns against having complicated points schemes, it raises the possibility of having a scheme in which households are placed in broad 'needs bands' which are used to help determine priorities when assessing responses to advertisements.

Housing allocations: what should be monitored

✔ The proportions of different ethnic groups that are offered and let dwellings, compared with the proportions on the housing register/transfer list or the proportions in need in the community as a whole

✔ Comparisons of the length of time different ethnic groups wait, on average, for offers and lettings

✔ Comparison between the quality of housing offered and let to the different ethnic groups

✔ Local authority nominations made to RSLs and subsequent offers, lettings and refusals

✔ In the case of RSL lettings, a comparison of the ethnic profile of tenants let dwellings in new schemes with the forecast profile made by the RSL when bidding for funding

✔ Whether there are differences between the various minority ethnic groups in terms of allocation outcomes: offers, lettings and refusals

✔ An analysis of reasons why offers are refused, distinguishing between the ethnic origins of the applicants, including refusals of offers on the grounds of fear of racist harassment

✔ The workings of community or local lettings schemes – wherever possible outcomes should be compared with those in a similar area where lettings are based on normal needs criteria

✔ The effects of recent changes to the allocation scheme

✔ Patterns of movement of different ethnic groups between areas

❑ Dealing with anti-social behaviour

This section deals with anti-social behaviour in general, while the following section concerns behaviour that is motivated by racism. Housing organisations should have clear policies and procedures to deal with anti-social behaviour and, as with the rest of their responsibilities, action should take into account differences in the needs and cultures of people from black and minority ethnic communities.

In recent years, there has been an understandable increase in the attention paid by landlords to bad behaviour amongst tenants, their families and visitors and there is now a wider range of sanctions that can be used against perpetrators. Where complainants and alleged perpetrators are of different ethnic origins, housing organisations should take particular care to investigate whether complaints about anti-social behaviour could have a racial motivation. Racists could make 'trumped up' allegations against black and minority ethnic tenants as a way of harassing them.

Dealing with anti-social behaviour: what should be monitored

✔ Ethnic profiles of complainants, alleged perpetrators and those against whom action is taken

✔ Type of action taken against perpetrators

❑ Tackling racist harassment

Black and minority ethnic people are more likely to be the target of racist victimisation than other groups of people. Although a large number of housing organisations have well defined policies and procedures to tackle racist harassment, recent research suggests that such policies are not as victim-centred as they should be (Chahal and Julienne, 1999). Victims are usually the first people to be lost in the procedure. They feel ignored, isolated and unsupported from not only the agency (or agencies) to which they have reported, but also from friends and family.

Chahal and Julienne found that racist harassment has a major impact on people's lives and becomes part of their routine everyday experience. People tend not to report harassment immediately, but only after a number of incidents have occurred. However, when they look for action, they find that the agencies to which they complain are incident-led. This creates a conflict between the course of action the complainant wants and what is provided. When individuals look for support, they find a piecemeal response and victims often develop their own strategies to manage the problem.

■ Principles of developing a policy

Housing organisations should develop policies that:

- Adopt the definition of racist incidents put forward in the Lawrence Inquiry report (see below)

- Enable the organisation to take swift and effective action against perpetrators with the aim of protecting the victim, stopping the harassment and preventing further incidents
- Reassure all victims and potential victims that action will be taken, and send a clear message to perpetrators
- Allow all residents to live peacefully, free from violence
- Develop preventative strategies
- Include a multi-agency approach
- Monitor the number of incidents and action taken

Organisations need to be aware that racist harassment may not only be targeted at people who belong to minority groups who are visible because of their skin colour. For example, Irish and Jewish people and people from Eastern Europe can experience racist harassment.

Policies on racist harassment should be part of a wider strategy for challenging nuisance and anti-social behaviour, regardless of whether housing organisations feel there is a problem or not.

Local authorities' anti-racist harassment strategies should not only address harassment in the authorities' own stock of rented housing. They should also cover leasehold housing, private housing, hostels and other forms of temporary accommodation.

There is a variety of sources of information that provide detailed information on how strategies can be developed to tackle racist harassment, support victims and interview perpetrators (for example Lemos, 1993; Lemos, 1997; Seager and Jeffery, 1994; Positive Action in Housing, Chartered Institute of Housing in Scotland and Scottish Homes, 1997). The CIH *Housing Management Standards Manual* also contains a useful checklist of good practice points.

A new online directory on action on racist harassment is due to be launched in autumn 2000. Known as RaceActionNet, and funded by several national agencies, the website will include details of good practice collected from 70 local authority areas.

The approach of the housing organisation should be victim-centred. This means that the people making the complaint are believed. They should be consulted and informed about how to proceed with the complaint and a course of action should be agreed with them.

■ The Stephen Lawrence Inquiry

The report of the inquiry into the death of Stephen Lawrence recommended that a new definition of a racist incident should be universally adopted by the police, local government and other relevant agencies:

> *'A racist incident is any incident which is perceived to be racist by the victim or any other person'* (Macpherson, 1999)

This definition means that if anyone – the victim, a witness, a police officer, or a housing officer – perceives an incident as racist, it should be recorded as such, regardless of any other views. The new definition is simple and clear and should help reduce the scope for failure to record racist incidents.

Other recommendations in the inquiry report are aimed at increasing reporting levels of racist incidents. They include:

- All racist incidents should be reported, recorded and investigated, whether or not a crime has been committed
- Co-operation between local agencies and local communities is needed in order to encourage people to report racist incidents – including facilities for reporting at any time of the day and at locations other than police stations
- Information about racist incidents should be shared widely
- Housing authorities, local schools and education authorities should record all racist incidents, report them to those who use their services and publish the information

The inquiry found that, whilst there were some examples of developing good practice, all too often housing organisations were seen to be slow and bureaucratic in their response to racist behaviour. In response to recommendation 15 of the Lawrence Inquiry report, the Home Office has published guidance on reporting and recording racist incidents (Home Office 2000a)

Many housing organisations have excellent anti-racist harassment policies and procedures. However, all of them need to ask if improvements could be made in their performance and their understanding of the impact of racism.

■ The Crime and Disorder Act 1998

The Crime and Disorder Act 1998 contains three areas of specific interest to organisations seeking to combat racist harassment.

Racially aggravated offences

The Act introduces a new concept of a racially aggravated offence. An offence will be held to be racially aggravated if the offender at the time of committing the offence, or immediately before or after doing so, demonstrates racial hostility towards the person experiencing harassment, or if the offence is motivated wholly or partly by racial hostility.

Anti-social behaviour orders

The Act contains provisions for anti-social behaviour orders (ASBOs). These are civil orders, similar to injunctions, for which the police or local authority, in consultation with each other, will be able to apply. The orders cover anti-social behaviour, defined as behaviour which causes, or is likely to cause, harassment, alarm or distress. The orders can be used to tackle low-level, persistent harassment, with the criminal law being used for more serious incidents.

Crime and disorder reduction partnerships

The Act places a new duty on local authorities and the police, along with a wide variety of other key players, to work in partnership to develop, at the local level, a crime and disorder reduction strategy. Strategies are required in each district, borough or unitary local authority area in England and Wales.

The views of black and minority ethnic communities should be fed into the crime and disorder reduction strategy. Anti-racist harassment multi agency panels are well placed to provide information on the level of racially motivated crime and how best to tackle racist harassment, and should be encouraged to play a full part in helping to develop the strategies.

Tackling racist harassment

The **London Borough of Croydon** Housing Department reviewed its procedures for dealing with racial harassment in 1997. This resulted in the launch of a new policy and procedures guide called *Guide to Action on Racial Harassment*, which emphasises the need to take all possible steps to prevent and tackle all forms of racial harassment.

The new policy was developed as a result of wide consultation with community organisations, households which had previously experienced harassment, the police and individuals and agencies working in this field elsewhere. All front line staff received training and new publicity was produced.

In 1999/2000, legal action was taken either by the council or by the police (using evidence and statements supplied by the council) in 11 cases. The council's use of injunctions has been particularly effective, and is applied to perpetrators living in the private sector as well as social housing.

Generally, a 'tool-box' approach is adopted, which emphasises the need for staff to support those who experience harassment and to work out an appropriate plan of action with them. In all cases, the role of housing officers is to provide regular contact and support to those experiencing harassment and to advise them of other forms of support and assistance in the community. The council has also been involved in the launch of a new community-based support service.

The council is committed to continuous monitoring and review of its procedures for dealing with harassment. All cases are monitored. Officers report annually to members and tenants panels on the cases dealt with and the action taken. There are regular strategy group meetings involving the police and RSLs, and the housing department takes a leading role in the corporate and multi-agency working groups.

A further review of current procedures has recently been undertaken which has recommended various measures for strengthening the council's work in this area. A new programme of staff training is being implemented and revised publicity material produced. All local RSLs have signed up to a protocol which sets out the minimum standards expected of social landlords in dealing with racist harassment and an agreement to share information on cases.

Leicester City Council provides community alarms to enable victims of harassment to summon help in an emergency. The council has agreed with the police that alarms installed for racist harassment and domestic violence will receive a grade one (the highest priority) response from the police.

A review of the service is carried out four months after the alarm has been installed. If there have been further incidents of harassment, the alarm remains in place. If there have been no incidents for 12 weeks prior to the review, either the alarm is removed or the household is charged for continuation of the service – the current rate (June 2000) is £1.60 a week.

Survey results

Tackling racist harassment

- Overall, 62% of authorities have written policies and procedures to tackle racist harassment in housing estates/areas. All but one authority where the black and minority ethnic population is 10% or more have written policies and procedures

- Where authorities have written policies and procedures, in 93% of cases they cover the authority's own rented homes (where they have them). In fewer areas the policies and procedures cover hostels (64%), other rented homes (31%) and owner occupied homes (25%)

- Authorities were asked to say who would normally be informed of an individual incident of racist harassment. The most frequently mentioned people/organisations to receive reports are: senior managers (84%), the police (74%), multi agency anti-racist harassment group (34%) and victim support scheme (28%).

- Not all authorities were able to say how many incidents of racist harassment had been reported in the last three years. Overall, 26% of authorities could not give a figure. Of the authorities with written racist harassment policies and procedures, 29% could not give a figure

- Only 20% of authorities have, or are carrying out, a review of policies and procedures in the light of recommendations of the Stephen Lawrence Inquiry report

■ Strategies to prevent racist harassment

Housing organisations can contribute to the prevention of racist harassment in a variety of ways:

- All tenants, residents and licensees should be informed of the organisation's policy on racist harassment and of the action that will be taken against perpetrators

- Careful publicity of action actually taken against perpetrators may help to deter others

- Advice, training and financial assistance provided to tenants' and residents' associations can help them to develop their own stance on racist harassment and can help them support victims and ensure black and minority ethnic residents participate in local activities

- Community development work can help raise awareness of the issues and support victims

- Improvements can be made to the security and design of dwellings in order to reduce crime

- Personal contact with recent movers can quickly establish if they are experiencing any problems. Early action can then prevent a situation escalating.

■ 'No harassment' clause in tenancy agreements

Including a 'no harassment' clause in the tenancy agreement sends a very clear message to all tenants that the organisation is serious about its commitment to dealing with anti-social behaviour. The legal procedures differ for changing the terms of existing secure and assured tenancies, but in each case the landlord is required to consult current tenants. This is an opportunity to raise awareness of the issue of racist harassment, as well as ensuring tenants understand the purpose of the clause. When new tenants sign their tenancy agreement, this clause, and the racist harassment policy, should be clearly explained.

Tackling racist harassment

Three organisations in Scotland have worked together to produce model procedures to tackle racist harassment. The procedures include committee responsibilities, investigating complaints, interviewing complainants, witnesses and alleged perpetrators, ongoing contact with complainants and legal remedies (Positive Action in Housing, Chartered Institute of Housing in Scotland and Scottish Homes, 1997).

A suitably worded 'no harassment' clause in a tenancy agreement allows an organisation to take legal action where their dwelling is associated with racist harassment, even where the tenant is not considered to be a perpetrator, for example where their children, other relatives, or visitors are perpetrators.

■ Joint working

Complaints of racist harassment are often not communicated to other agencies (Chahal and Julienne, 1999). A multi-agency approach is fundamental when developing and implementing racist harassment procedures. Housing organisations should be involved with any local multi-agency initiative that exists.

It is also essential that there is effective communication within organisations to ensure that cases are dealt with in an efficient, effective and supportive manner. Staff who draw up policies and procedures need to work closely with the front line staff who will be implementing the policies. Housing staff will need to liaise with colleagues in social services/social work, education departments and community development teams. Contact with a range of agencies is crucial because, for example, the racist harassment reported may involve children (both as victims and perpetrators). Each agency needs to maintain lists of identified contacts within a range of services and agencies. These should be updated on a regular basis.

The Social Exclusion Unit's report on *Anti-social Behaviour* (Policy Action Team 8), recommends that local Crime and Disorder Partnership strategies should include a statement of intent to tackle racist harassment and a plan setting out what each agency will do. The strategies should include a protocol for reporting and recording racist incidents. Protocols should include specific and transparent arrangements for sharing information about racist incidents and perpetrators (Social Exclusion Unit, 2000c).

Tackling racist harassment

The **London Borough of Camden's** Anti-Social Behaviour Action Group (ASBAG) comprises a co-ordinator, specialist solicitor, administrator and racial harassment co-ordinator. The group plays a lead role in the local multi-agency response to harassment and has appointed a Sylheti-speaking racial harassment caseworker. Initiatives include:

Anti-harassment charter: The charter was launched in July 1997 and sets out the council's commitment to taking firm action against the perpetrators of harassment while providing individually tailored support packages for victims. The charter is available in the main languages used in the borough.

Victim support package: Victim support packages are available to council tenants/leaseholders who have experienced harassment. The packages reflect the needs of individuals and can include:
- Referrals to appropriate counselling/support agencies
- Emergency repairs and graffiti removal
- Extra security facilities as appropriate, for example fireproof letterboxes, new window and door locks and surveillance visits from the mobile security patrol
- Help with interpreting/translation

24-hour harassment helpline: The 24-hour harassment hotline incorporates a multi-lingual help facility.

Inter-agency training: A programme of inter-agency training for local police and housing officers was provided during 1998. As a direct result of the training, Neighbourhood Action Partnerships (NAPs) were set up, which operate at both strategic and practical levels. At the strategic level, meetings are held between sector inspectors and district managers, and other partners as relevant, to decide where resources should be directed and how their use may be maximised. At the practical level, the emphasis is on implementation.

Protocol agreements: The council, in partnership with the police, has drawn up several protocols, or confidentiality agreements, to enable casework and information exchange. The protocol system ensures that all parties know exactly what is required of them, and takes away the discretionary element as it consolidates the way information is shared.

Quality circles: Several quality circles were established in early 1999. The aim is to seek the views of black and minority ethnic residents and assess their levels of satisfaction with how the council and the police have dealt with their cases in the past, and also whether they are currently suffering from any type of anti-social behaviour.

Following the publication of the Stephen Lawrence Inquiry report, the **City & County of Swansea** convened an inter-agency meeting to discuss a response to the report's recommendations. From that meeting, it was clear that there was much good practice currently within the area, but there was scope for sharing good practice and developing inter-agency training. The Crime & Disorder Partnership was asked to include training, research into racially motivated crime and community safety issues as part of its local action plan.

Prior to the publication of the report, the issue of racially motivated crime was being addressed by the Swansea Bay Multi Agency Forum on Racial Attacks and Harassment. The Forum is made up of a number of organisations, including: the City & County of Swansea, the police, Victim Support, the Racial Equality Council, the probation service, Neath Port Talbot County Borough Council and the Crown Prosecution Service.

The Forum operates at three levels:

- Policy making and co-ordinating the activities of the various agencies
- An initiatives group which implements the policy forum's decisions
- A casework forum which co-ordinates the response to specific racist incidents

The Forum has adopted the Stephen Lawrence Inquiry report definition of a racist incident. All participating agencies use a common notification form to report individual incidents.

Bradford MDC and the **Bradford Racial Equality Council** took the lead in forming the Bradford Alliance against Racial Harassment, a partnership which includes the police, the Probation Service, Victim Support and the Crown Prosecution Service. The aim of the alliance is to involve community based organisations in taking an active role in identifying and challenging racist harassment.

As a first step, a network of community based confidential reporting centres has been set up thoughout the district. These centres will often be the first port of call for victims to get help and they aim to give victims the confidence to come forward, so that their problems can be tackled in an atmosphere that is accessible and trusting. The functions of these centres include:

- Receiving complaints and recording information on a central database
- Providing, or referring victims for, support and counselling
- Providing or facilitating diversionary activities in order to encourage cross-cultural social contact
- Acting as a direct link for local communities and the statutory sector

■ Monitoring performance

There is now a new Audit Commission performance indicator within the 'corporate health' group of indicators relating to racist harassment. It concerns the number of 'racial incidents' recorded by the authority per 100,000 population. Racial incidents are any incidents regarded as such by the victim or anyone else. The indicator applies both to services and employment (DETR, 1999b).

The Social Exclusion Unit's report on *Anti-social Behaviour* (2000c) recommends that the recording of racist incidents should be included in the Best Value performance indicators and that targets should be set for the reduction of such incidents, both locally and nationally.

Tackling racist harassment: what should be monitored

✔ Ethnic origin of victims and perpetrators

✔ Location of reported incidents

✔ Refusals of offers of dwellings because of fear of racist harassment

✔ Any changes in the level of reported incidents following publicity campaigns

✔ Action taken against perpetrators

✔ Support provided to victims

❑ Repairs and improvements

Black and minority ethnic people may suffer disadvantage in repair and maintenance services because:

- They may be less aware than their white counterparts about their landlords' repairing obligations and policies and so may not report some repairs that are outstanding.

- Communication difficulties may result in the landlord not recording properly what repair needs doing, or the tenant may not fully understand the landlord's communications, for example about repairs programmes or appointment times.

- Where women are in the house without male adult household members present, they may be reluctant to admit male repair inspectors or operatives. Consequently, repairs may be delayed or cancelled altogether.

Housing organisations need to take care when communicating important pieces of information about repairs, particularly if there are serious consequences for the tenant if he or she does not respond in the way required, for example a cancelled repair order. Organisations should consider translating documents that give important information to tenants about the repairs they have ordered. The use of information sheets with 'exploded' diagrams of dwelling elements and fittings may help tenants to indicate what repair needs doing. Organisations should seek to recruit more inspectors and operatives who can speak other languages.

Repair inspectors and operatives should be trained so that they understand the particular sensitivities that exist in some cultures about women coming into contact with male strangers. Where difficulties are encountered, employees should be instructed to arrange a further visit at a time when a male adult will be at home. The recruitment of more female inspectors and operatives and the introduction of appointment systems, so that tenants know in advance when someone will be calling, should also help to reduce the problem.

Women's repair team

Leicester City Council has a women's repair team. It was originally set up to carry out repairs to the homes of women who had suffered domestic violence. The service has now been extended and, if a woman requests the services of the team, then this will be provided if possible. The service is open to all women council tenants and to hostels.

The team consists of 13 operatives and covers a number of trades: carpentry, plumbing, painting, bricklaying, plastering and gas fitting.

Attention also needs to be focused on improvement and major repair schemes. There is some evidence that black and minority ethnic people do not benefit proportionately from investment in the social housing stock (Law, Davies, Phillips and Harrison, 1996). Housing organisations need to have clear, objective criteria for selecting areas of their housing for investment. Stock condition surveys based on a representative sample of dwellings are a good starting point for investment strategies. Improvement and major repair programmes should be included in ethnic monitoring arrangements.

Repairs and improvements: what should be monitored

- ✔ A breakdown of the ethnic origin of tenants reporting repairs in a particular period compared with a breakdown of the ethnic origin of all tenants
- ✔ Comparisons between the various ethnic groups of the organisation's response time for particular categories of repairs
- ✔ Comparisons between the various ethnic groups of the levels of satisfaction with the repair service
- ✔ Ethnic profiles of residents living in areas where improvements or major repairs are carried out

Key questions

- *Have Best Value reviews taken account of the need to provide appropriate services to tenants and potential tenants from black and minority ethnic communities?*

- *Have proposed changes to housing allocation schemes been carefully modelled to make sure that the effects of the changes will not discriminate against black and minority ethnic people?*

- *Has the definition of a racist incident set out in the Lawrence Inquiry report been adopted, and have policy and procedures for tackling racist harassment been reviewed in the light of the report's recommendations?*

- *Do tenancy agreements feature non-harassment clauses, and are the implications of these highlighted at tenancy sign-up?*

CHAPTER 6

WORKING WITH OTHER ORGANISATIONS

This chapter examines how race equality principles should underpin the working arrangements that exist between local authorities, RSLs, voluntary organisations and contractors.

❏ Partnerships between local authorities and RSLs

As important providers of social housing and, in many areas, key players in area regeneration, RSLs are central to delivering the objectives of a black and minority ethnic housing strategy. In England, RSLs are specifically encouraged by the Housing Corporation to work within the policy framework set by local authorities for meeting black and minority ethnic needs (Housing Corporation, 1998).

■ Meeting black and minority ethnic needs

Local authorities are responsible for assessing housing needs, including the needs of black and minority ethnic communities, and for setting priorities for funding programmes. Where they consider that there are unmet needs amongst the minority communities, authorities should ensure that RSLs are aware of these so that they can consider whether, and how, they can respond. Some authorities publish an annual statement of needs and priorities they wish RSLs to address. In Scotland, joint agreements between local authorities and Scottish Homes provide the framework in which black and minority ethnic needs can be met by social landlords.

Local authorities are often involved in deciding, in conjunction with the Housing Corporation/Scottish Homes/the National Assembly for Wales, which RSLs should be involved in major projects in their area, such as regeneration schemes or the development of large sites. Choosing partners involves taking account of a variety of factors – RSLs have a range of skills and experience to offer and the final decision about partners will involve a balanced judgement of some kind. There should, however, be a 'baseline' standard in relation to race equality. Local authorities should introduce into the selection process methods for assessing the extent to which RSLs are putting race equality principles into practice in the way they deliver their services. Where projects involve provision that is targeted at black and minority ethnic communities, selection methods should specifically seek to establish how far the RSLs' day to day services will be appropriate – for example, whether they employ staff with appropriate language skills, whether literature is translated, whether they have experience of participation initiatives that involve black and minority ethnic tenants and so on. Specific consideration should be given to the need to involve black and minority ethnic RSLs.

■ Getting 'race' on to the agenda

In many areas, there are formal structures for local authorities and RSLs to consult each other, usually involving consultative forums and working groups. Race equality issues should take their rightful place on the agenda, and forums could address, as appropriate:

- Exchanging information about black and minority ethnic needs and, where appropriate, jointly commissioning research into needs

- Monitoring progress in providing for black and minority ethnic needs, for example monitoring investment targets against outcomes

- Reviewing information from the monitoring, by ethnic origin, of nominations and nomination outcomes

- Exchanging details of local good practice, for example on tackling racist harassment or consulting black and minority ethnic communities

- Considering the need for joint projects, such as multi-agency racist harassment projects or interpreting/translating services

■ Black and minority ethnic RSLs

Black and minority ethnic RSLs are important providers of housing and have been supported by two five-year Housing Corporation strategies. A black and minority ethnic RSL is one where at least 80% of the governing body is drawn from black and minority ethnic communities. There are now 64 such landlords registered with the Housing Corporation and together they own or manage 21,000 dwellings in England.

In Scotland, there are two black and minority ethnic RSLs, both based in Glasgow. Between them they are responsible for just over 600 dwellings. The proposed Scottish Homes race equality strategy supports the development of further such RSLs. At present, there are no black and minority ethnic RSLs in Wales. However, the recently published report on the need for a Welsh black and minority ethnic housing strategy recommends that the National Assembly for Wales should consider the need for a black and minority RSL (Nyoni, 2000).

Black and minority ethnic RSLs have had a substantial impact in England. An evaluation of the Housing Corporation's strategy for black and minority ethnic RSLs carried out in 1996 found that there were no equivalent programmes in Europe, North America or Australia. The review also found that these landlords had:

- Made a valuable contribution to identifying and meeting needs
- Provided opportunities for black and minority ethnic people to participate in policy making and management
- Provided role models for the communities they served
- Influenced housing agency practice across the social housing sector
- Made major contributions to links with social care and to 'housing plus' and economic regeneration
                          (Harrison, Karmani, Law, Phillips and Ravetz 1996)

In addition to these contributions, many black and minority ethnic RSLs have strong links with local communities. White-led housing organisations should, in partnership, use these links to facilitate community consultation or to market the services they provide.

Black and minority ethnic RSLs often work in partnership with other RSLs in delivering the housing strategy locally. Useful advice about developing such partnerships is set out in the Federation of Black Housing Organisation's guide on working together. The guide sets out 13 good practice points about partnership working:

- Research your partner
- Do not give up at the first hurdle
- Similarity of objectives
- Commitment to the partnership
- Setting out terms of reference
- Keep lines of communication open
- Get legal advice
- Shop around

- Mutual support and recognition
- Equality between partners
- Flexibility – keep your options open
- Retain your independence
- Prepare yourself for the partnership

(Julienne and Straker, 1998)

All RSLs seeking to grow and develop need the support of the local authorities in whose areas they wish to work, and black and minority ethnic RSLs are no exception. While maintaining a competitive environment, local authorities' strategies for partnership should take particular account of black and minority ethnic RSLs and should recognise the expertise these landlords have built up. Even though there is no national target for the proportion of the Housing Corporation Approval Development Programme to go to schemes provided by black and minority ethnic RSLs in England, some local authorities continue to agree local targets with regional offices of the Housing Corporation, as a way of recognising the specific role the RSLs can play.

Because of their relatively small size, it is difficult for many black and minority ethnic RSLs to compete on an equal basis with large white-led social landlords. Where local authorities are facilitating the development of large schemes, they should actively consider breaking the development down into more manageable sections, or perhaps stipulating that developers must work in partnership with a black and minority ethnic RSL on part of the development.

The rate of transfer of housing stock by local authorities is gathering pace. The role that black and minority ethnic RSLs can play in such transfers should be fully recognised. The Housing Corporation has said that such landlords should be actively involved in these developments, where appropriate, and that it will liaise with local authorities to consider any barriers to their involvement that might exist (Housing Corporation, 1998). Where local authorities own housing in multi-racial areas, they may wish to consider the merits of transfers to existing black and minority ethnic RSLs, which may already be managing housing in those areas. There may also be scope for establishing new black and minority ethnic RSLs to receive transferred stock.

The Housing Green Paper (DETR, 2000c) stresses the opportunity provided by stock transfer to improve the diversity of housing management, and recommends that local authorities pursuing this route consider the transfer of ownership or management of part of their stock to community-based and black and minority ethnic-led RSLs, with the full involvement of local people.

Apart from the argument that black and minority ethnic RSLs should be in a better position to provide more appropriate services to minority communities, there may also be other advantages arising from such transfers. In a recent study of the way English RSLs in general are meeting the needs of black and minority ethnic communities, Tomlins et al (2000) point to an example of where a RSL transferred part of its stock to a black and minority ethnic RSL. Previously all the transferring RSL's tenants had been white, but after the transfer, it managed to attract black and minority ethnic tenants into the stock it retained in management.

Other ways in which local authorities can support black and minority ethnic RSLs are by:

- Supporting their bids for funding
- Selling them land or buildings for renovation
- Providing capital or revenue funding for schemes to meet identified needs
- Seconding staff to them

Many local authorities take account of rents (often for existing homes as well as proposed rents for new developments) when making decisions about which RSL they wish to work with in particular schemes and which bids to support for funding. Some black and minority ethnic RSLs charge rents which are higher than those charged by white-led social landlords for similar properties. There are a number of reasons for this, particularly the fact that the housing stock of black and minority ethnic RSLs is newer on average than that of white-led landlords, and was largely developed under mixed funding regimes. However, it is important to note that, recently, black and minority ethnic RSLs have kept their rent increases below the average for all RSLs (Housing Corporation, 2000). To ensure that communities can benefit from having active black and minority ethnic RSLs in their areas, it is important that local authorities take a balanced approach to partner selection and to bids. Without doubt, rent levels are extremely important and affordable rents are essential to the achievement of the government's Welfare to Work policies. But local authorities should be careful not to rule out partnership with a black and minority ethnic RSL on the basis of rent levels alone, and should take into account other factors, including the appropriateness of the services that will be provided and the contribution the RSL will make to wider regeneration objectives.

In any event, local authorities will need to be working with RSLs, including black and minority ethnic RSLs, to achieve greater coherence in rent structures as set out in the Housing Green Paper.

Survey results

Working with other organisations

- 57% of authorities said that, when choosing which partner organisations should be involved in delivering local housing services and programmes, account is taken of the organisations' race equality policy and procedures.

- 44% of non-stock transfer authorities said that account is taken of companies' race equality policy and procedures when choosing contractors.

- Mostly, organisations are judged by looking at their written equal opportunities policy documents.

- Of the 51 authorities which have black and minority ethnic RSLs working in their areas, 69% said they have policies or programmes to work with these RSLs. The most commonly mentioned methods of joint work were: requiring white-led RSLs to work with them, transfer of stock to them and providing revenue funding.

- Of the 75 authorities which have black and minority ethnic community and voluntary organisations working in their area, 81% had policies and programmes to work with them. Joint projects (for example on racist harassment), providing funding, or free use of, or reduced rent on, local authority buildings were the most commonly mentioned methods of joint working.

- Of all non-stock transfer authorities, only 5% have taken any specific initiative to facilitate the employment of black and minority ethnic contractors.

❏ Working with black and minority ethnic voluntary organisations

Voluntary organisations can often provide services that are more sensitive to need than those provided by statutory bodies. Other potential advantages can be lower overheads, flexibility and ability to innovate.

In drawing up black and minority ethnic housing strategies, full account should be taken of the role that black and minority ethnic led voluntary organisations can play. Their contribution could be:

- Helping mainstream organisations to consult effectively, by facilitating access to black and minority ethnic communities.

- Providing services that are targeted at black and minority ethnic communities, for example services for homeless people or those with care and support needs, or helping to tackle anti-social behaviour. These services can be provided through service level agreements or similar arrangements with the commissioning organisation.

- Advising mainstream organisations on how their services can be made more sensitive to black and minority ethnic communities and helping the organisations to market and publicise services within the communities.

Voluntary organisations cannot of course be expected to provide these services free of charge and adequate funding from the commissioning organisation will be required. Apart from funding, other ways in which housing organisations can work with black and minority ethnic organisations include:

- Seconding staff
- Providing training for their employees and committee members
- Making available housing stock for management, for example properties or small groups of dwellings could be managed by voluntary organisations as supported housing schemes
- Providing free, or subsidised, office space

Recognising the degree of disadvantage faced by many black and minority ethnic communities as a result of past discrimination, local authorities could consider targeting a proportion of their funding programmes for black and minority ethnic led organisations. Funding programmes also need to be flexible and there should be regular reviews of priorities and funding criteria. It should be possible to fund innovative projects and those that respond to newly discovered need. Without flexibility, older well-established organisations may benefit disproportionately at the expense of newer groups.

Working with voluntary organisations: what should be monitored

✔ Comparison between the success rates of grant applications from black and minority ethnic voluntary organisations with applications from mainstream organisations

✔ Comparison between the proportion of grant paid to black and minority ethnic organisations and the proportions black and minority ethnic people make up of the population in the district

❑ Employing contractors

Housing organisations obtain many of the services they require through the use of outside contractors and, particularly in the case of larger organisations, they have considerable 'spending power' within the local economy. Many organisations have an active policy of maximising the use they make of companies run by people from black and minority ethnic communities. It is good practice to set a target for the proportion of an organisation's purchasing that is obtained from black and minority ethnic suppliers, and to regularly monitor progress against the target.

Housing organisations should make sure that their dealings with contractors are based on race equality principles. There are three dimensions to this:

- The methods organisations use for appointing contractors should not unfairly discriminate against black and minority ethnic contractors, and opportunities for using the services of these contractors should be created

- All contractors should comply with basic equality of opportunity standards in relation to their employment practices

- The services that are provided by contractors should embody equality principles

■ Fairness to black and minority ethnic contractors

Housing organisations need to recognise that, although their methods for purchasing goods and services may seem ostensibly fair and non-discriminatory, they could be unwittingly denying opportunities to black and minority ethnic run contractors. Barriers to access to contracts by black and minority ethnic organisations, and possible ways of overcoming them, are set out below:

- Some housing organisations may not be aware of the businesses that are run by people from black and minority ethnic communities in their area.
  Is there a local directory of black businesses? In areas where no such directory exists, is there a need for such a directory to be compiled?

- Contracts may be unnecessarily large. Black and minority ethnic contractors may not be big enough to take on the contract.
  Could the contract be divided up in some way into more manageable portions whilst maintaining value for money? Should main contractors be encouraged to subcontract part of the work to black and minority ethnic contractors?

- Black and minority ethnic contractors may not have the 'track record' of experience to convince the commissioning organisation that they can do the job.
  Is it possible for black and minority ethnic contractors to be awarded small contracts outside the formal tendering requirements (most organisations have more flexible arrangements for contracts under a certain value) to enable them to gain the necessary experience?

- Smaller contractors may find the tendering process too daunting and the conditions too onerous.
  Can tendering procedures be simplified and are there unnecessary conditions which can be removed? Can housing organisations get together to run a local project to help black and minority ethnic contractors meet tendering requirements?

- Payment schedules may create cash flow problems for small contractors.
  Can commissioning organisations provide payments at more frequent intervals throughout a contract and take steps to reduce delays between receiving an invoice and making the payment?

Promoting the use of black and minority ethnic contractors

The **London Equal Opportunities Federation** exists to promote enterprises run by black and minority ethnic people, women and people with disabilities. Organisations eligible to affiliate to the Federation include local authorities, RSLs, health authorities and trusts, government bodies and other not for profit organisations. Among the commitments of affiliation are that organisations must:

- Play an active role in promoting the aims of the Federation, in particular the aim of promoting use of the enterprises run by people from black and minority ethnic communities, women and people with disabilities that are on the Federation's register
- Set achievable and measurable targets for the use of enterprises that are on the register
- Review tender list management processes in order to ensure that they allow new business relationships to develop
- Provide feedback to the Federation on the use of minority-led businesses

Contracting with enterprises that are on the Federation's register means that organisations can be assured that the contractors meet industry standards, have the relevant insurance, the appropriate legal and tax status and are supported by independently supplied references.

In December 1999 the Federation launched a new code of practice, with the support of the DETR, the Department of Trade and Industry, the Local Government Association and other organisations. The code of practice clarifies the measures that need to be taken by local authorities, RSLs and other organisations to achieve equal opportunities in contract awarding and commissioning practice.

This has been taken forward through the completion of *Contracts of Exclusion*, a research project commissioned by the Housing Corporation under its black and minority ethnic housing policy.

The Federation has also launched the register online, at www.safebuild.com, and is in negotiation with the Housing Corporation and Constructionline over the provision of a complete Egan-compliant system for users, which will also enable users to identify and appoint minority-led construction businesses.

■ Ensuring all contractors comply with equal opportunity standards in relation to employment practices

Local authorities are legally obliged to carry out their responsibilities for contracting without reference to non-commercial matters. However, under the Local Government Act 1988, they are able to satisfy themselves that organisations with which they contract, or from which they receive tenders or applications to be included on tender lists, are taking reasonable steps to eliminate unlawful racial discrimination and to provide equal opportunities in the field of employment. Authorities are permitted to ask companies seeking entry to tender lists six questions about the steps they take to avoid discrimination and to promote equal opportunities.

The six questions relate to:

1. Whether it is the company's policy to comply, as an employer, with the Race Relations Act

2. Whether there has been a finding of unlawful racial discrimination against the company in the last three years

3. Whether in the last three years the company has been formally investigated by the CRE

4. Steps taken in response to any finding or investigation under 2 or 3 above

5. Whether the company's policy on race relations is set out in certain specified documents

6. Whether, as far as possible, the company observes the Commission's Code of Practice in Employment

In addition to equality issues relating to the selection of contractors, local authorities are recommended by the CRE (1995c) to set standards for race equality which contractors must meet. These standards should be based on compliance with the Race Relations Act 1976 and the Commission's Code of Practice in Employment (CRE, 1984). Contract conditions can be used to set out the requirements a local authority will make of an employer in relation to equal opportunities and will allow the authority to monitor the employer's performance. The CRE's publication (1995c) *Racial Equality and Council Contractors* contains model contract conditions, detailed advice about the selection process using the six questions and how contracts should be monitored.

Employing contractors: what should be monitored

✔ Number and value of contracts let to black and minority ethnic contractors

■ Providing services embodying equality principles

Housing organisations are responsible for making sure that contractors deliver services embodying race equality principles. The specification – the document defining and describing the service that contractors are to provide – is central to this process. Great care is needed to make sure that the specification covers the full range of equality issues considered important by the organisation, since contractors cannot be forced to do things that are not in the specification, and it may prove difficult and expensive to revise the specification once the contract is running.

Targets for the employment of black and minority ethnic people

The **London Borough of Southwark** has a local labour agreement that applies within the Peckham Partnership Single Regeneration Budget area.

Within the overall Peckham Partnership targets, there is a section dealing with the numbers of local construction jobs created. The current target for scheme completion is 576 construction jobs, of which 324 are anticipated to be filled by people from black and minority ethnic communities. The actual figures monitored to date are 356 jobs, of which 161 are filled by people from black and minority ethnic communities. Targets are set at the start of each year and are monitored quarterly and reported to the Government Office for London.

As part of the New Deal for Communities programme, the Aylesbury regeneration scheme will also include a local labour agreement. This will be agreed within the next two years when work is due to start, and it is likely that the targets will be similar to those in the Peckham Partnership.

In the private sector, the council's Private Housing Renewal Unit aims to encourage contractors from all ethnic backgrounds to be involved in regeneration activities. Between 1996 and the present, a total of 71 contractors were used on renovation grant works and, of these, 14 were from black and minority ethnic communities. The Private Housing Renewal Unit provides residents with a list of contractors who regularly carry out grant works and this list includes black and minority ethnic builders.

The Local Government Management Board (1995) suggests that specification writers ask themselves a number of questions about the service that will help to identify equality issues. These questions can be summarised as follows:

- Is the service accessible?
- Is the service appropriate to the needs of different user groups?
- Is there clear information about the service?
- What are user consultation and complaints procedures?
- What are the equalities record-keeping systems?
- Have conditions relating to the need for a competent, sufficient and supervised workforce been included?
- Have health and safety, including non-harassment, been considered?

Having awarded a contract to a particular supplier, it is important to monitor how the contractor is performing. Checking out compliance with equality requirements should be integral to the overall monitoring process. The Local

Government Management Board (1995) recommends a number of methods of monitoring:

- Reports from contractors
- Service statistics
- Complaints
- User involvement and feedback
- Site visits and inspections on a random basis
- Meetings with the contractors

Key questions

- *Have policies and procedures for choosing partners and contractors been reviewed recently? Are race equality principles written into the procedures?*

- *Has enough consideration been given to the important role that black and minority ethnic RSLs and voluntary organisations can play in providing services locally?*

- *Are race equality issues given a high enough profile in consultative arrangements between local authorities, RSLs and other organisations?*

CHAPTER 7

MONITORING AND EVALUATION

This chapter discusses ways in which black and minority ethnic
strategies should be monitored and evaluated, and in particular looks at
the importance of involving the community in the monitoring process.
It also outlines key principles and some practical issues relating to
ethnic record keeping and monitoring.

❑ The importance of monitoring and evaluation

Monitoring and evaluation are essential to any strategy. Without them, it is
not possible to know whether the strategy is achieving the intended changes.
They can provide information that might help to reveal why failure may be
occurring, where responsibility for difficulties may lie and, crucially, what
can be done to refine the strategy to make it more successful.

If the strategy is linked to a realistic action plan, outcomes can be set against
targets and even small incremental changes can be measured. It is important
to set in place internal and external monitoring procedures: internal
monitoring may be the responsibility of a core group of officers, while
external monitoring is a crucial part of local accountability and may involve
feeding back to the community what has been achieved over an agreed
period.

Monitoring and evaluation are key activities within the Best Value regime.
Best Value provides a positive role for communities in reviewing services, a
framework for measuring how far organisations are achieving targets and a
stimulus to continuous improvement in services. The CRE's guidance
Auditing for Equality (1999) aims to help local authorities audit their
performance against the five levels set out in *Racial Equality Means Quality*.

Chapter 2 identified the need for the strategy to contain clear objectives
following consultation with the communities affected and with the partners
that are to be involved in delivering the strategy. It is essential that:

- Objectives are clearly defined and are based on the aims of the strategy

- Tools are in place to measure how far objectives have been achieved
- The impact of the strategy on the achievement of objectives can be measured and, as far as possible, the impact of other, 'non-strategy' variables (such as things that would have happened anyway) can be isolated

Annual review of the strategy

One of the ways in which **Rochdale MBC** reviews its Housing Strategy for Asian Communities (see page 31) is by holding an annual conference to which representatives from a wide range of statutory and voluntary organisations are invited.

The conference held in March 2000 received a detailed report on progress on the action plan which formed part of the strategy. Amongst other issues, the report detailed:

- Successes – the targets which had been achieved or exceeded
- Targets not achieved – reasons why the target had not been achieved were stated and a revised target for the following year was set

As well as reviewing progress on targets included in the original strategy, conference participants are encouraged to suggest new initiatives to be included in the action plan for the forthcoming year. Part of the value of the conference is that it motivates all those involved in implementing the strategy and is planned as a high profile event – in 2000 the Home Office Minister Mike O'Brien attended as a speaker.

❏ Involving partners and communities in evaluation

The implementation of a black and minority ethnic housing strategy will inevitably involve a partnership between different organisations. It is important that monitoring and evaluation techniques are able to measure the performance of the various organisations contributing to achieving strategic objectives. It is therefore vital for partner organisations to be involved in the design of monitoring and evaluation methods, and, in addition, they should take part in collecting the data for, and in helping to interpret the results of, monitoring and evaluation exercises.

Representatives of the communities the strategy is seeking to benefit also have an important role to play. It would be discourteous, to say the least, if community representatives were only consulted when the strategy was being developed, but were not informed of how the strategy was working out in practice. Even more important, communities should be involved in the evaluation process itself. Their perspective can demonstrate how policies are working out 'on the ground'.

There is a variety of ways to obtain the community's perspective on the way the strategy is working:

- Using existing consultative mechanisms – for example residents' forums or panels
- Specially conducted surveys
- Public meetings
- Focus groups

❑ Monitoring, evaluation and continuous improvement

The black and minority ethnic strategy should set out how monitoring and evaluation will be carried out. It is important to consider:

- How often is routine monitoring of objectives and targets to be carried out?
- At what stage will a thorough evaluation be conducted?
- Who is to carry out the monitoring and evaluation?
- Who will receive monitoring and evaluation reports?

Thought needs to be given to evaluation when the strategy is being designed. Concentrating on measures of success will help refine the strategy's objectives and components. Early consideration of the proposed approach to evaluation will also help identify practical issues, such as whether a 'before' study should be carried out, or whether new data collection systems are required.

There is a strong argument for an independent evaluation of the strategy at some stage. The independent body chosen to carry this out should have the skills to talk to all parties involved, including the black and minority ethnic communities, and be able to make a detached assessment.

Evaluation is not a static process. Successes should be built on. New, more exacting, targets can be set in order to achieve year on year improvement in services. Failures should lead to questioning about the causes, and indeed about whether the target was right in the first place. An unmet target, perhaps refined in the light of the lessons learned, can be 'carried forward' into the next implementation period with a renewed commitment to achieving it.

More detail about evaluation techniques can be found in the CIH/LGA Good Practice Guide on local housing strategies (Goss and Blackaby, 1998).

❑ Ethnic record keeping and monitoring

■ Principles

Ethnic monitoring involves collecting, analysing and reporting information on processes, outputs and outcomes in a way that distinguishes between the ethnicity of different groups and which enables comparisons to be drawn between the experiences of different groups or between targets and outcomes. Ethnic monitoring is vital to the overall monitoring and evaluation of a black and minority ethnic housing strategy.

The CRE's handbook on ethnic monitoring *Accounting for Equality* outlines seven principles of ethnic monitoring:

- Consultation – to gain public trust and confidence
- Confidentiality – it should not be possible to identify individuals
- Self-classification – individuals should decide for themselves which ethnic group they belong to
- Effectiveness – the system must be clearly defined, staff must be trained, performance measures must be set and response rates must be monitored
- Monitoring – ethnic records must be monitored regularly
- Action – problems revealed by monitoring reports should be followed up by action
- Accountability – regular reports should be produced and made available publicly

(CRE, 1991b)

Survey results

Monitoring employment and training

✎ 88% of authorities keep ethnic records of applicants for jobs. 71% keep records of those shortlisted and 72% keep records of those who take up employment.

✎ Only 28% keep ethnic records of those receiving training, 27% keep records of those leaving the employment of the authority and 21% keep records of those who are disciplined.

✎ Many authorities do not regularly analyse the ethnic records they keep. For example, 37% do not analyse, at least once a year, their records on applicants for jobs.

The points made in the CRE's handbook about monitoring, action and accountability are important. The postal survey of local authorities has shown that a significant number of authorities do not analyse the data they collect and also that many do not report the results to significant stakeholders, including councillors. It is pointless, and somewhat dishonest, to ask those applying for, or receiving, services to supply details of their ethnic origin, and then do nothing with the data that is collected.

Survey results

Reporting and using the results of ethnic monitoring

- Authorities were asked who receives monitoring reports regularly (at least once a year). Only 39% of authorities that keep ethnic records of services report the results to councillors and only 43% of authorities that keep employment ethnic records report the results to councillors.

- Of all authorities that keep ethnic records on services for tenants/potential tenants, 29% said they have made changes over the last five years to the services as a result of ethnic monitoring. Of all authorities that keep ethnic records of other services, 21% said they have made changes, over the last five years, to their strategy or services as a result of ethnic monitoring.

- Changes that have been made include becoming aware of the needs of black and minority ethnic groups, reviews of racist harassment policies and procedures, building more larger homes and the introduction of lettings targets.

- Of all authorities that keep employment ethnic records, 26% said that, in the last five years, they have made changes to their employment or training policies as a result of ethnic monitoring.

- Changes that have been made include the introduction of training programmes, the preparation of an equal opportunities policy, the setting of recruitment targets and recruiting of black and minority ethnic people to PATH schemes.

■ The scope of ethnic monitoring

For local authorities, the scope of ethnic monitoring should extend beyond their role as landlords. Many people within the black and minority ethnic communities look to sectors other than council housing to meet their needs and it is important that there is monitoring of services to people outside the council sector, as well as services to those within it. Of significance to particular black and minority ethnic communities are the house renovation grant service, the route to RSL tenancies via local authority nominations and enforcement activities in the private rented sector.

The study by Tomlins et al (2000) of English RSLs found that the scope of ethnic monitoring currently being carried out by RSLs is somewhat limited, with relatively few going beyond the requirements of the Housing Corporation and of the CORE system. The authors state that it would appear that this limited activity will prevent many RSLs from moving towards a more proactive approach to policy review within the Best Value regime.

Survey results

Monitoring services for tenants and potential tenants

- 81% of authorities keep ethnic records of their housing registers and 76% keep ethnic records of their transfer lists. However, only 50% of authorities keep ethnic records of those to whom dwellings are let. Only 11% analyse records on the length of time that different ethnic groups wait for a home, whilst only 6% analyse the quality of homes let to the different groups.

- 55% of authorities keep records of the ethnic origin of racist harassment victims and 37% keep records of racist harassment perpetrators.

- Many authorities do not regularly analyse the ethnic records they keep. For example, 44% do not analyse, at least once a year, their housing register records and 42% do not analyse, at least once a year, their transfer list records.

Note: Stock transfer authorities are excluded from the above figures

---

The precise scope of ethnic monitoring should reflect circumstances locally. Many organisations will start with monitoring housing allocations and recruitment and then prioritise other areas, using judgement about where discrimination is most likely to be occurring. Chapters 3 – 6 contain a number of checklists of topics that should be monitored.

Local authorities, RSLs and housing voluntary organisations should seek to use the same ethnic origin classifications. The introduction of new ethnic origin categories in the 2001 Census provides an ideal opportunity to adopt a standard approach. The main changes to be introduced in 2001 are the introduction of an Irish category (in England and Wales) and a number of mixed race categories.

Survey results

Monitoring other services and activities

✏ 79% of authorities keep ethnic records of homeless applicants and 59% keep ethnic records of nominations to RSLs. However, only 33% keep ethnic records of lettings by RSLs.

✏ Only 26% of authorities keep ethnic records of house renovation grant applicants, 27% keep ethnic records of people seeking housing advice and 5% keep ethnic records of contractors and consultants who are employed.

✏ Many authorities do not regularly analyse the ethnic records they keep. For example, half of authorities do not analyse at least once a year their homeless applicant records.

■ Using the data

It is useful to classify ethnic monitoring data in three ways:

- **Descriptive.** An example of descriptive data would be a table showing the number of lettings being made over a period of time to households in the various ethnic groups. On its own, descriptive data is of limited use because it does not show whether what is happening is satisfactory or not

- **Comparative.** This data compares two or more sets of information. For example, the proportion of lettings being made to various ethnic groups can be compared with the proportion that each group represents amongst those applying for accommodation. Differences between the lettings and applications profiles should trigger questions about whether priority systems are correct and whether housing that is appropriate in terms of needs and preferences is being offered. Other examples of comparative data include comparisons between the quality of homes let to different ethnic groups and comparisons in waiting times between the application for a renovation grant and grant approval. Comparisons over time can also be helpful. For example, an ethnic breakdown of service users, which is produced regularly over a period of time, can help measure the effectiveness of outreach and promotion activities.

- **Performance.** This data compares outcomes with a target or standard. Targets set out an expectation of performance. They are not quotas and neither do they represent attempts at positive discrimination (CRE, 1991b). Targets can be set, for example, on the proportion of lettings that should be made to various ethnic groups over the period of a year, based on information about their needs. Performance against the targets should be regularly monitored. A failure to meet a target must not be used as an excuse deliberately to manipulate housing allocation decisions – that could well amount to unlawful discrimination. But failures to meet targets should prompt discussions about priority systems, the effectiveness of communication and whether current services are appropriate. The level of the targets themselves should be regularly reviewed.

Survey results

Comparing performance

✎ 18% of authorities have, over the last three years, compared their performance in the field of housing and race equality against some external standard or benchmark. 43% of authorities in areas where the black and minority ethnic population is 10% or more have compared their performance.

✎ Of those authorities that do compare, the standards against which they most frequently compare their performance are the CRE's standard, with other local authorities and with RSLs.

The CRE's handbook gives further practical guidance on collecting, analysing and presenting monitoring data and on where the responsibilities for effective ethnic monitoring should lie.

Key questions

- *Does the black and minority ethnic housing strategy contain targets that lend themselves to systematic measurement?*

- *Are communities and partners involved in evaluating the black and minority ethnic housing strategy?*

- *Are ethnic records analysed and reported regularly to councillors or the board of management? Are monitoring reports made available to the general public?*

- *Have ethnic origin categories been reviewed in the light of the new categories proposed for the 2001 Census?*

CHAPTER 8

CONCLUSIONS

The environment in which local authorities, RSLs and other housing organisations work is changing. These changes present ideal opportunities for policies and services to be reviewed. The challenges created by Best Value should be used to examine critically whether principles of fairness and equality of opportunity are given sufficient priority in the way that services are currently delivered. The introduction of Tenant Compacts requires local authorities to develop inclusive approaches to participation and involvement. The devolved administrations in Scotland, Wales and Northern Ireland, and the new equal opportunities legislation in Northern Ireland, all create new opportunities for fresh thinking on approaches to race equality.

It is hoped that this Guide is of use to all local authorities, RSLs and other housing organisations – whether they have done a lot of work in the field of 'race' or whether they are only just starting to get to grips with the issues.

The approach to race equality set out in this Guide could be summarised as follows:

- Recognition of the diversity of communities
- Consultation with the communities about needs and preferences, recognising that diversity will require a variety of approaches
- Analysis of information about the communities, which could include new research or interpretation of existing data
- Designing policy responses – new services, changes to existing services or new partnerships – which are sensitive to the diversity of need and which are outcome-oriented
- Evaluation and monitoring of policies and programmes, leading to changes in approach, where needed, and building on the successes that have already been achieved.

Over a year after the publication of the Lawrence Inquiry report, when progress is being reviewed, the focus is still very much on reform – new thinking about the way issues of 'race' are approached, legislation to strengthen the statutory framework and recognition of the need for each organisation to carry out a thorough examination of its approach to race equality.

The challenges that face those who manage and work for housing organisations are as real as those that exist in the police force and in other services. The time is right for change. It is hoped that this publication can provide some of the practical guidance needed to make change possible.

REFERENCES AND FURTHER READING

Anwar, Muhammad (1996) *British Pakistanis: Demographic, Social and Economic Position*, Centre for Research in Ethnic Relations, University of Warwick

Argent, K, Carter, S and Durr, P (2000) *Facing Reality: Evolving Responses by London Boroughs to Racial Harassment*, London Housing Unit

Ashram Agency (1997) *A Culture of Care: A Guide to Culturally Sensitive Design and Care in Sheltered Housing for Frail Asian Elders*

Asylum Rights Campaign (1999) *Out of Sight Out of Mind – A Report on the Dispersal of Asylum Seekers in the UK*

Beishon, S, Modood, T and Virdee, S (1998) *Ethnic Minority Families*, Policy Studies Institute

Berthoud, R (1998) *Incomes of Ethnic Minorities*, University of Essex

Berthoud, R (1999) *Young Caribbean Men and the Labour Market: A Comparison with Other Ethnic Groups*, Joseph Rowntree Foundation

Bonnerjea, L and Lawton, J (1998*) No Racial Harassment This Week*, Policy Studies Institute

Bowes, A, Dar, N and Sim, D (1998) *Too White, Too Rough and Too Many Problems: A Study of Pakistani Housing in Britain*, University of Stirling

Brownhill, S and Darke, J (1998) *Rich Mix: Inclusive Strategies for Urban Regeneration*, Policy Press

Carter, S (1998) *Hidden Crisis: A Study of Black and Minority Ethnic Homelessness in London*, Frontline Housing Advice Ltd

Chahal, Kusminder (2000) *Ethnic Diversity, Neighbourhoods and Housing, Foundations,* Joseph Rowntree Foundation

Chahal, Kusminder and Julienne, Louis (1999) *We Can't All Be White! Racist Victimisation in the UK,* Joseph Rowntree Foundation

Chartered Institute of Housing (1999) *Good Practice Briefing: Housing and Services for People with Support Needs*

Chartered Institute of Housing (2000) *Housing Management Standards Manual*

Chartered Institute of Housing/Local Government Association (1998-2000) *Housing and Best Value: A Guidance Manual*

Clark, Vernon (1994) *Getting Black Tenants Involved: A Good Practice Guide for Housing Associations and Co-operatives,* CATCH

Cole, Ian, Hickman, Paul, Millward, Liz and Reid, Barbara (1999) *Developing Good Practice in Tenant Participation,* Department of the Environment Transport and the Regions

Commission for Racial Equality (1984) *Race Relations Code of Practice for the Elimination of Racial Discrimination and the Promotion of Equality in Employment*

Commission for Racial Equality (1991a) *Training: Implementing Racial Equality at Work*

Commission for Racial Equality (1991b) *Accounting for Equality: a Handbook on Ethnic Monitoring in Housing*

Commission for Racial Equality (1991c) *Race Relations Code of Practice in Rented Housing*

Commission for Racial Equality (1992) *Race Relations Code of Practice in Non-Rented (Owner-Occupied) Housing*

Commission for Racial Equality (1993) *Room for All: Tenants Associations and Racial Equality*

Commission for Racial Equality (1995a) *Racial Equality Means Business: A Standard for Racial Equality for Employers*

Commission for Racial Equality (1995b) *Racial Equality Means Quality: A Standard for Racial Equality for Local Government in Scotland*

Commission for Racial Equality (1995c) *Racial Equality and Council Contractors*

Commission for Racial Equality (1996) *Racial Equality Means Quality: A Standard for Racial Equality for Local Government in England and Wales*

Commission for Racial Equality (1997) *Race, Culture and Community Care: An Agenda for Action*

Commission for Racial Equality (1999) *Auditing for Equality: Auditing Council Performance against the Commission for Racial Equality's Standard for Local Government 'Racial Equality Means Quality'*

Cooper, J and Qureshi, T (1993) *Through Patterns Not Our Own: A Study of the Regulation of Racial Violence on the Council Estates of East London*, University of East London

Croydon People's Housing Association (1999) *Our Voices: A Community Consultation Report*

Daly, G (1996) *Homelessness*: *Policies, Strategies and Lives on the Street*, Routledge

Department of the Environment, Transport and the Regions (1998) *English House Condition Survey*

Department of the Environment, Transport and the Regions (1999a) *Circular 10/99 Local Government Act 1999: Part 1 Best Value*

Department of the Environment, Transport and the Regions (1999b) *Best Value and Audit Commission Performance Indicators for 2000/2001*

Department of the Environment, Transport and the Regions (1999c) *Housing Management: Effective Housing Management in the Most Deprived Areas*, Report of Policy Action Team 5*

Department of the Environment, Transport and the Regions (1999d) *National Framework for Tenant Participation Compacts*

Department of the Environment, Transport and the Regions (1999e) *Unpopular Housing*, Report of Policy Action Team 7*

Department of the Environment, Transport and the Regions (2000a) *Best Value in Housing Framework*

Department of the Environment, Transport and the Regions (2000b) *New Deal for Communities Race Equality Guidance*

Department of the Environment, Transport and the Regions and Department of Social Security (2000c) *Quality and Choice: a Decent Home for All,* The Housing Green Paper

Department of the Environment, Transport and the Regions (2000d) *Local Housing Needs Assessment: A Guide to Good Practice*

Department of Land Economy, University of Cambridge (1998) *Evaluation of the SRB Challenge Fund: A Partnership for Regeneration,* Department of the Environment, Transport and the Regions

Dorsett, R (1998) *Ethnic Minorities in the Inner City*, Policy Press

Federation of Black Housing Organisations and Barnardos (1995) *Black Homelessness in South Wales*

Federation of Black Housing Organisations and University of Cambridge (1996) *Black Housing Associations and Private Finance: A Good Practice Guide*

Goss, Sue and Blackaby, Bob (1998) *Designing Local Housing Strategies: A Good Practice Guide*, Chartered Institute of Housing and Local Government Association

Harrison, M, Karmani A, Law, I, Phillips, D and Ravetz, A (1996) *Black and Minority Ethnic Housing Associations*, Research 16, Housing Corporation

Hawtin, Murray, Kettle, Jane, Moran, Celia and Crossley, Richard (1999) *Housing Integration and Resident Participation: Evaluation of a Project to Help Integrate Black and Minority Ethnic Tenants,* York Publishing Services for the Joseph Rowntree Foundation

Hickman, Mary and Walter, Bronwen (1997) *Discrimination and the Irish Community in Britain,* Commission for Racial Equality

Home Office (2000a) *Code of Practice on reporting and recording racist incidents in response to recommendation 15 of the Stephen Lawrence Inquiry Report*

Home Office (2000b) *Race Equality in Public Services – Driving Up Standards and Accounting for Progress*

Housing Corporation (1997) *Performance Standards and Regulatory Guidance for Registered Social Landlords*

Housing Corporation (1998) *Black and Minority Ethnic Housing Policy*

Housing Corporation (1999) *Guidelines for Registered Social Landlords on the Provision of Housing and Support Services for Asylum Seekers*

Housing Corporation (2000) *Corporation News*, January 2000, Issue 76

Housing Corporation, North West and Merseyside Regional Office (1999*) Black and Minority Ethnic Housing Strategy in the North West and Merseyside*

Jeffrey, Joanna and Seager, Richard (1995) *All Together Now: Involving Black Tenants in Housing Management*, Tenants' Participation Advisory Service

Jones, Adrian (1994) *The Numbers Game: Black and Minority Ethnic Elders and Sheltered Accommodation*, Anchor Housing Trust

Julienne, Louis and Straker, Leroy (1998) *Best Value in Partnerships: Social Housing Landlords Working Together*, Federation of Black Housing Organisations

Karmi, G (1996) *The Ethnic Health Handbook*, Blackwell Science

Karn, Valerie, Mian, Sameera, Brown, Mark and Dale, Angela (1999) *Tradition, Change and Diversity: Understanding the Housing Needs of Minority Ethnic Groups in Manchester*, Housing Corporation

Karn, V and Phillips, D (1998) *Race and Ethnicity in Housing* in Blackstone, T, Parekh, B and Saunders, P (eds) *Race Relations in Britain*, Routledge

Law, I (1996) *Racism, Ethnicity and Social Policy*, Prentice

Law, I, Davies, J, Phillips, D and Harrison, M (1996) *Equity and Difference: Racial and Ethnic Inequalities in Housing Needs and Housing Investment in Leeds*, University of Leeds

Lee, Peter and Murie, Alan (1997) *Poverty, Housing Tenure and Social Exclusion*, The Policy Press

Lemos, Gerard (1993) *Interviewing Perpetrators of Racial Harassment: A Guide for Housing Managers*, Lemos Associates

Lemos, Gerard (1997) *Safe as Houses: A Guide to Supporting People Experiencing Racial Harassment in Housing*, Lemos and Crane

Local Government Management Board (1995) *Equalities and the Contract Culture*

London Research Centre and Lemos and Crane (1998) *Assessing Black and Minority Ethnic Housing Needs*, Housing Corporation

Macpherson, W (1999) *The Stephen Lawrence Inquiry: Report of an Inquiry by Sir William Macpherson of Cluny*, Cm 4262-I, HMSO

Modood, T, Berthoud, R, Lakey, J, Nazroo, J, Smith, P, Virdee, S, Beishon, S, (1997) *Ethnic Minorities in Britain: Diversity and Disadvantage,* Policy Studies Institute

National Housing Federation (1998) *Race Equality in Access to Housing Services: A Good Practice Guide*

National Housing Federation and Home Housing Trust (1998) *Accommodating Diversity: Housing Design in a Multicultural Society*

Nyoni, Mutale (2000) *From the Margins to the Centre: Assessing the Need for a Black and Minority Ethnic Housing Strategy in Wales*, National Assembly for Wales

O'Mahoney, B and Ferguson, D M, (1991) *Young, Black and Homeless in London*, Barnados

PATH LA (1997) *Tenth Anniversary Report*

Positive Action in Housing (1999) *Promoting Choice and Opportunities in Housing for Older People from Black and Ethnic Minority Communities*

Positive Action in Housing, Chartered Institute of Housing in Scotland and Scottish Homes (1997) *Tackling Racial Attacks and Harassment: Model Procedures for Scottish Housing Providers*

Randall, Geoffrey and Brown, Susan (1997) *Meeting the Need: Irish Housing Associations in Action*, Housing Corporation and Housing Associations Charitable Trust

Robertson, Douglas and McLaughlin, Pat (1996) *Looking into Housing: A Practical Guide to Housing Research*, Chartered Institute of Housing

Scottish Office (1999) *Partners in Participation: The National Strategy for Tenant Participation*

Scottish Homes and Scottish Federation of Housing Associations (1999) *Performance Standards for Registered Social Landlords*

Scottish Homes (1999) *Performance Standards and Regulatory Guidance for Registered Social Landlords*

Scottish Homes (2000) *Action for Race Equality: Consultation Paper*

Seager, Richard and Jeffery, Joanna (1993) *Housing Black and Minority Ethnic Elders*, Federation of Black Housing Organisations

Seager, Richard and Jeffrey, Joanna (1994) *Eliminating Racial Harassment: A Guide to Housing Policies and Procedures*, Lemos Associates

Smaje, C (1995) *Health, 'Race' and Ethnicity: Making Sense of the Evidence*, King's Fund Institute

Small, C and Hinton, T (1997) *Reaching Out: A Study of Black and Minority Ethnic Single Homelessness and Access to Primary Health Care*, Health Action for Homeless People

Social Exclusion Unit (1998) *Bringing Britain Together: A National Strategy for Neighbourhood Renewal*, The Stationery Office*

Social Exclusion Unit (2000a) *National Strategy for Neighbourhood Renewal. A Framework for Consultation*, The Stationery Office*

Social Exclusion Unit (2000b) *Neighbourhood Management*, Report of Policy Action Team 4, The Stationery Office*

Social Exclusion Unit (2000c) *Anti-social Behaviour*, Report of Policy Action Team 8, The Stationery Office*

Social Exclusion Unit (2000d) *Minority Ethnic Issues in Social Exclusion and Neighbourhood Renewal*, The Stationery Office*

Tai Cymru (1997) *Regulatory Requirements for Registered Social Landlords in Wales*

Tenants' Participation Advisory Service (England) (1993) *Keynote Number 6: Equal Opportunities for Tenants Associations*

Tenants' Participation Advisory Service (England) (1994) *Working Together: Involving Black Tenants in Tenant Participation*

Tomlins, et al (2000, forthcoming) *Meeting the Needs of Local Black and Minority Ethnic Communities: A Study of Registered Social Landlords*, The Housing Corporation

Welsh Office (1999) *Local Housing Needs Assessment*

Wood, Peter and Preston, Jill (1997) *Assessing Housing Need: A Guidance Manual*, Scottish Office Development Department

Zetter, R and Pearl, M, (1999a) *Guidelines for Registered Social Landlords on the Provision of Housing and Support Services for Asylum Seekers within the Framework of the 1999 Immigration and Asylum Legislation and the Transitional Arrangements*, Housing Corporation

Zetter, Roger and Pearl, Martyn (1999b) *Managing to Survive: Asylum Seekers, Refugees and Access to Social Housing*, The Policy Press

* Policy Action Team and other SEU reports can be obtained via the Social Exclusion Unit website www.cabinet-office.gov.uk/seu